INDEX

ON CENSORSHIP

INDEX ON CENSORSHIP 1 1999

WEBSITE NEWS UPDATED EVERY TWO WEEKS
www.indexoncensorship.org
contact@indexoncensorship.org
tel: 0171-278 2313
fax: 0171-278 1878

Volume 28 No 1 January/February 1999 Issue 186

Index on Censorship (ISSN 0306-4220) is published bi-monthly by a non-profit-making company: Writers & Scholars International Ltd, Lancaster House, 33 Islington High Street, London N1 9LH. *Index on Censorship* is associated with Writers & Scholars Educational Trust, registered charity number 325003 *Periodicals postage*: (US subscribers only) paid at Newark, New Jersey. Postmaster: send US address changes to *Index on Censorship* c/o Mercury Airfreight International Ltd Inc, 365 Blair Road, Avenel, NJ 07001, USA
© This selection Writers & Scholars International Ltd, London 1999
© Contributors to this issue, except where otherwise indicated

Subscriptions (6 issues per annum)
Individuals: UK £39, US $52, rest of world £45
Institutions: UK £44, US $80, rest of world £50
Speak to Tony Callaghan on 0171 278 2313

EDITORIAL

Turning points

Time and again, political considerations have taken precedence over justice. We had good reason to think they would again. This time, despite accusations of naivety or piety levelled at the human rights world, it was different. The UK law lords may have overturned their first judgement that General Pinochet has no immunity against charges of torture, hostage-taking and conspiracy to murder, but some things have changed for ever. Previous heads of state responsible for gross violations of human rights are going to make more cautious travel plans in future. There will be pressure to change the law on immunity if Pinochet is returned to Chile; to seek an earlier ratification of the International Criminal Court; to create a new climate of accountability for crimes against humanity.

We were told repeatedly by the likes of Norman Lamont, Margaret Thatcher and Chris Patten – how bizarre that attitudes to Pinochet should have taken such crudely party political lines in the UK – that his arrest would have catastrophic consequences for democracy in Chile. Others, within that country, say that, on the contrary, it could be the making of what is still a precarious and inconclusive political compromise. David Lehman describes Chile today as 'a postmodern nightmare ... school psychologists routinely adminster the drug Ritalin to class room troublemakers – by which is meant anyone who asks questions too often ... the poor and the rich barely cross paths at all ... the Chilean constitution is in many ways a mockery'.

The issues of truth and reconciliation in Chile have been left unresolved: suppressed memories and deep, unhealed wounds leave a legacy of unease and fear (*Index* 5/1996). Those who argue that the Pinochet case should never have been brought are simply arguing for more papering over of the cracks. Democracies that do not properly confront their past become crippled.

But legacies of unease deriving from concealment have other sources too. This issue of *Index* looks at the return of Macau to China and, with it, the end of the last historic European empire. Portugal sowed a strange species of self doubt in its colonies: united by language, many of them adopted neo-colonial governments that complied with western realities and took on a received identity that had little to do with their own cultures or peoples. Our Brazilian country file reflects this – a country at pains to present itself as a colour-blind democracy while in reality still struggling with the legacy of slavery.

contents

LETTERS

The Scientology view

From Bill Walsh, Human Rights Counsel, and Martin Weightman, Director, Church of Scientology European Human Rights Office

The statements concerning Scientology and Germany in 'Sect Crime' (*Index* 3/98) are replete with untruths, half-truths, contrived mis-statements and wholly unwarranted characterisations devoid of fact – all calculated to justify Germany's deplorable human rights record by casting a minority religion in a false light. Such propaganda has no place in a human rights publication and requires a response to set the record straight regarding serious human rights violations directed against minorities in Germany.

Scientologists in Germany continue to be routinely dismissed from jobs, dismissed from private schools, dismissed from political parties, dismissed from professional associations, sports and social organisations, denied the right to licences, denied the right to bank accounts and loans, denied the right to perform or exhibit art, denied the right to rent public facilities, denied the right to join social, political or professional organisations, and denied the right to contract with or be employed by the government.

The German government has urged all strata of society to ostracise Scientologists by economically blacklisting anyone associated with Scientology. This is illustrated by so-called 'sect filter' clauses in contracts recommended by the government. Such clauses have been adopted or promoted by the Permanent Conference of Ministers and Senators of Interior of the States, by state governments in Bavaria, Hamburg, Berlin and Baden-Württemburg, by the major political parties, and by federal ministers in the previous government such as Minister of Family Affairs Claudia Nolte and Minister of Labour Norbert Bluem, who called for a ban of all Scientologists from occupations which 'intersect with society,' including schools, the government and business companies.

This government policy mandates that any private organisation doing business with the government institute its own blacklisting policy or risk retaliation. For example, the Bavarian government requires businesses contracting with it to swear that no employees of the company 'use the technology of L. Ron Hubbard.' This forces corporations to adopt the government's exclusionary policy toward Scientologists or suffer serious economic consequences.

As a result, the use of these 'sect filter' clauses in the private sector has become shockingly systematic throughout Germany. There are hundreds of documented cases of Scientologists who are routinely fired or not hired when they are confronted with these clauses and refuse to sign them. These 'filters' are deliberately designed to require an individual to either declare his religious beliefs and be punished for them by being blacklisted or boycotted or publicly denounce such beliefs under threat of economic sanctions. This policy is manifestly illegal and contrary to international human rights instruments by directly violating the 'untouchable core' of the right to freedom of conscience and belief by penalising people for holding certain beliefs. The atmosphere of hate created by the former government has led to bomb threats, death threats, and other hate crimes directed at German Scientologists.

The author's attempt to downplay these serious human rights violations which have ruined the lives of many Scientologists in Germany, flies in the face of approximately 20 human rights reports by independent and objective bodies on the subject. For example, the United Nations Human Rights Committee, in its annual report published in September 1997, expressed its concern that actions taken to exclude Scientologists from public service employment violated Germany's international human rights obligations. The United Nations Special Rapporteur on Religious Intolerance has also reported on these violations over the last four years. The Helsinki Commission held hearings in September 1997 on religious intolerance in which extensive testimony was received regarding a government policy of religious discrimination in Germany against Muslims, Scientologists, Charismatic Christians, Jehovah's Witnesses, and other targeted minority faiths. Other authorities, including a special Ad Hoc Committee, composed of United Kingdom religious, political and academic figures, have cited Germany for its policy of minority religious discrimination against Scientologists, Jehovah's Witnesses, and other minority faiths.

Indeed, the definitive 1997 world study by the University of Essex Human Rights Centre, *Freedom of Religion and Belief: A World Report*, details extensive cases of human rights violations directed at Scientologists in Germany. This highly acclaimed and respected study finds: 'In Germany, democracy is used as an ideology to impose conformity. It has been dismaying to discover that the state, and some of its politicians and people, are using what are known from the past to be well-worn paths of discrimination and intolerance and of inciting of intolerance towards a new religious minority, the Scientologists.'

The authors' cannot justify these violations by wild and unsupported claims that Scientology intends to 'overthrow the government' and that 'Scientologists 'control a large share of real estate in Hamburg.' Scientology never has had a political agenda. Anyone familiar with Scientology knows that it operates as a peaceful, apolitical religious institution in over 120 countries and that Scientology parishioners are known as law-abiding citizens who contribute to the betterment of democratic communities throughout the globe. The notion that 30,000 German Scientologists, less than .0003% of the German population, constitutes a political threat represents a paranoia which cannot bear scrutiny. Likewise, the Church owns one property in all of Germany in contrast to the Catholic and Lutheran Churches, which together own 4 billion square metres of real estate.

Regarding Scientology's religious nature – numerous internationally recognised scholars have independently studied Scientology beliefs and practices and agree that it is a bona fide religion. Moreover, international human rights authorities such as the United Nations Human Rights Committee and a body of religious experts convened by the Organisation for Security and Cooperation in Europe have directed states not to discriminate against religions that are 'newly established or represent religious minorities that may be the subject of hostility by a predominant religious community'.

Germany should be striving to protect religious freedom for all instead of mounting campaigns to demonise members of minority religions to justify human rights violations. Hopefully, the new government will change Germany's course by looking at the facts instead of the propaganda and embrace a policy of minority religious tolerance.

Captain Euro hits back
From Nicolas De Santis, President, Twelve Stars

Elizabeth Prest's article on Captain Euro (*Index* 5th/98)

surprised me greatly, particularly the allegations that we are 'blissfully ignorant of Europe's past'.

My family suffered greatly at the hands of extremists in Italy and Spain. My father was beaten and tortured by the Nazis in Rome; my mother fought for democracy in Spain during the Franco regime and suffered accordingly; my grandmother, pregnant at the time, was hung by her feet, tortured and imprisoned for three years by Franco's police for her efforts to combat such extremism. It is my belief that, through greater European integration, the horrors of fascism and extremist forms of nationalism that have affected my family and millions of others will be banished once and for all.

Over eight years of research and preparation went into this project. Captain Euro is simply a cartoon superhero communicating to the people of Europe, not just the UK, the benefits that can be derived from greater unity and the adoption of the single currency.

I do sincerely hope that once the single currency has been launched, the British people will see the benefits of uniting more with their fellow Europeans and leave behind the extremists that continue to distort the true reality and future of Europe.

A step back for Ireland?

From Maggie Beirne, Research and Policy Officer, Committee on the Administration of Justice

Far be it from me to suggest censorship to the editor of Index on Censorship, but I was somewhat surprised at the comments of Michael Foley and John O'Farrell about the introduction of emergency measures in the wake of Omagh. In their article (*Index* 5th/98) they conclude that, despite some criticisms of the civil liberty implications, 'most people have accepted that extraordinary events demand extraordinary measures and that draconian legislation, possibly even internment without trial, is a price they must pay to defend democracy'. I will be writing to John, whom I know, to refute this argument, but perhaps *Index* should encourage a broader debate about such a contention? After all, this assertion about Britain would presumably not pass unremarked if it were said about Turkey or Serbia.

Previous statements made by CAJ with the Irish Council for Civil Liberties (both before and after the passage of this legislation) sum up our concerns. ICCl spokesperson Michael Farrell said: 'The response by the Irish government is reminiscent of the actions taken by Britain in the wake of the Birmingham bombings over 25 years ago. We should remember that those departures from the rule of law led to miscarriages of justice and the imprisonment of people like the Birmingham Six and the Guildford Four, while those responsible remained free. While governments have a responsibility to bring perpetrators to justice, they need to be sure that their response is in conformity with internationally protected human rights.'

We argue, as we have regularly argued, that it is human rights abuses that have fed and fuelled the conflict, and that it is generally accepted by international commentators that emergency powers breed human rights abuses. Our analysis of the reaction to Omagh therefore is the exact opposite of John's and Michael's: we would say that democracy will be undermined, not defended, by this retrograde step. Apart from being a violation of basic rights, it is politically counter-productive.

Cheap and offensive

From Lawrence Elliot

I have been a devoted reader of Index on Censorship from its

inaugural issue, and a subscriber since almost immediately after, so please know that I write as a friend when I say that I found your 5th/98 cover pathetically obvious and cheap and breathtakingly offensive. Surely there remain less puerile ways of attracting the public notice to a valid point than aping the Murdoch press?

And suppose Mr Blair felt free to respond in kind: what would your reaction be, Ms Owen, to a Soviet-style cleverly-cropped photo of you in your underwear?

Glad to oblige. I'm sorry you found our cover offensive. We feel it belongs to a fine tradition of satirical cartoons. Bending a manifesto commitment to Freedom of Information is more offensive than poking digital fun at the man doing the bending...
UO

news

in the

● **Dictator of the month** *Politika*, the biggest circulation Yugoslav daily, published the results of an opinion poll that asked: 'Who is your favourite foreign public figure?' Belarus President Alyaksandr Lukashenka, distinguished for his less than progressive views on things like freedom, democracy and the role of the media, headed the list of distinguished nominees with an overwhelming majority.

● **Pole faulting** Totem poles erected to help beautify Port Moresby in Papua New Guinea have come under scrutiny from the country's censorship board. The depiction of genitals and sexual acts as carved on the traditional poles are, they claim, classified as obscene under the present Censorship Act.

● **The virgin and the comedian** On 3 November, one of Turkey's top comedians went on a one-day hunger strike after vowing to die unless censorship laws were changed. Levent Kirca was protesting against the state broadcasting commission's decision to shut down Kanal D television for 24 hours because the comedian made fun of a government minister who claimed she was still a virgin. Fellow comedians cancelled their TV shows in support of his campaign and marched on parliament. Human rights campaigners point out that this may not be the best issue on which to rally wide support: women's groups have condemned Kirca for ridiculing the women's affairs minister, Isilay Saygin, who said she was a virgin and proud of it.

● **Miss who?** On 16 October the director of the Miss Croatia pageant declared invalid the recent election of Lejla Sehovic, alleging there were 'voting irregularities' and that one vote was invalid. Sehovic, who is a Muslim, claimed the organisers opposed her election, and replaced her with a Croatian contestant, because of her religion. The dispute ended on 28 October when organisers ruled that Sehovic would represent the state in the 1998 Miss World Pageant, with the Croatian candidate filling the role in 1999.

● **Sleighbells in Havana** Santa Claus is no longer an enemy of the Revolution. Christmas is coming to Cuba for the first time since it was abolished as a public holiday almost 30 years ago. In the latest concession in their policy of religious *perestroika*, Cuba's Communist rulers declared that Santa Claus and nativity scenes will be allowed to return for good. '

● **Bad hair day** A teacher at Public School 75 in Brooklyn, New York, was removed from her classroom in late November after an uproar because she was teaching a book featuring a black girl with unruly hair. Ruth Sherman said she was using *Nappy Hair* – a semi-autobiographical story by Carolivia Herron, a black university professor of English – as a way of boosting self-esteem among black and latino students. The idea backfired when students and parents complained to Sherman's superiors.

● **Shaking things up** Dressed for the occasion in the gossamer, sequin-studded fabrics traditional in their trade, Israeli bellydancers demonstrated outside the foreign ministry building in Jerusalem on 12 November. Their complaint: charges of sexual assault were not being pressed against Egyptian Ambassador Mohammad Bassiouny because of his diplomatic immunity.

● **Viagra – again** The parliamentary committee for culture and information have criticised Egyptian State television for 'maligning the country's traditions' and 'overstepping the bounds of public decency'. The wonder drug Viagra was once again at the centre of controversy. MP Abdel Rahman Al Shehawi demanded that TV officials be held accountable for a programme in which the use of the drug was debated. The same committee also invited censorship officials to come over and discuss 'the rampant spread of indecent magazines in the bookshops'. This probe was prompted by a complaint lodged with the speaker Fathi Suror by a female student protesting the display of indecent magazines in Cairo shops.

● **No oil painting** Turkey's former President, Kenan Evren, went on trial on 22 October charged with plagiarism. The ex-general, who seized power in a coup in 1980, faces up to one year in jail for basing a painting on a photograph by Fikret Otyam without permission. His three years of military rule were marked by widespread detentions and long jail sentences of leftwing activists. In 1989, he retired to the sea to pursue his hobby of oil painting.

● **'Writs R them'** The proprietor of a small animal welfare charity in the UK has been threatened with legal action by the world's largest toy store chain. Toys 'R' Us say the name of Maryon Maychell's charity, Cats 'R' Us, could cause confusion. They have given her 14 days to change it. A Toys 'R' Us spokesman said that the company was only protecting its name and would be happy if Mrs Maychell changed the name to Cats Are Us.

● **Snookered** On 25 October, the *Independent on Sunday* reported that it was joining forces with the *Guardian* and BBC Radio 5 Live to protest the ban on UK snooker correspondent Clive Everton. Everton, one of the game's most prominent representatives, alleges that the World Professional Billiards and Snooker Association has denied him press facilities at tournaments because of his criticism of the way they run the game.

● **All Fcuked up** The Church of England and the Roman Catholic Church have combined to condemn ads by the UK fashion chain French Connection. Their letter to the chain's chief executive complains that ads displaying 'Fcuk Christmas' are 'repugnant and callous' to Christians and others who regard Christmas as special. French Connection have run into trouble before for the controversial use of their company initials.

● **Huntin', bettin' & smokin'** State referenda run in tandem with US mid-term elections in November covered a wide range of burning issues. In Alaska, Oregon, Washington, Nevada and Arizona, voters approved the medical use of cannabis; in Hawaii they said no to same-sex marriages; Californian voters came out in favour of legalised gambling; in Missouri they banned cock-fighting and bear-baiting; and Minnesota enshrined the right to hunt for sport in its constitution.

● **Where have all the voters gone** Up to 40 per cent of the next generation of black males in the USA could permanently lose the right to vote if current trends in crime rates continue. Almost every state denies prisoners the right to vote and 14 states do not allow offenders to vote even after they have served their sentence, a policy that disenfranchises more than 1 million. Any felony offence can trigger disenfranchisement: first-time offenders found guilty of one drug sale can lose their right to vote for life. Nearly 4 million

US adults have already lost the right to vote; 1.4 million of them are black men.

● **Lott of fuss** Sixty-five-year-old James Hormel lost his nomination as ambassador to Luxembourg in October when Senate majority leader Trent Lott refused to vote on his appointment. Hormel, heir to a meat-packing fortune, would have been the first openly gay US ambassador. Lott hit the headlines early in 1998 when he said gays were sinners who had much in common with alcoholics and kleptomaniacs.

● **Own goal** 22,000 police and paramilitary troops were on duty outside Galataseray football team's Ali Sami Yen stadium on 2 December for the European Champions' League match with Juventus of Italy. The match had already been postponed because of continuing anger in Turkey over Italy's refusal to extradite Kurdish rebel leader Abdullah Ocalan, but Anti-Italian sentiments were still running high with flag burnings, daily demonstrations across the country and calls for a boycott of Italian goods. Recalling the experience of Manchester United five years earlier, when they were received with banners proclaiming 'Welcome to Hell', Juventus were naturally unhappy about meeting Galataseray but said they felt obliged to play the match. In the event, it ended in a 1-1 draw with few incidents.

● **Pulp friction** Outgoing director of the British Board of Film Classification, James Ferman, said that with the benefit of hindsight he would have made cuts to the film *Pulp Fiction*. Ferman told the Institute for the Study of Drug Dependence that some of the scenes in the film were 'practically an advertisement' for heroin and that the film's director Quentin Tarantino was 'socially irresponsible'. Steve Rolles from Transform, the campaign for effective drug policy, said Ferman was right not to have cut the scenes: people do enjoy drugs and it wouldn't be honest not to show this.

● **Hold the front page** UK police in Kent have issued severe warnings to local newspapers about their racist, anti-immigrant rhetoric. They accuse the press of inciting violence, and have told at least one editor that his paper faces prosecution if it continues to publish what a force spokesman described as 'unacceptable' and 'inflammatory' reports. He blamed both the local press on the South coast and national tabloids, such as the *Sun* and the *Daily Mail,* which regularly take a strong anti-immigrant editorial line, for 'heightening tensions and attracting far-right groups, like the National Front'.

The warning is not before time. The *Dover Express* ran an editorial in which it listed asylum-seekers along with drug smugglers as 'the back-draft of the nation's sewage', under a headline which stated: 'We want to wash dross down the drain'. And when, several weeks ago, 103 Romanian men, women and children were found hiding in the back of a lorry at Dartford, the tabloids responded with an onslaught of negative articles about asylum seekers and refugees. Police were forced to deploy extra officers to protect refugees living in Dover, after two Slovaks had the door of their house set alight in what police suspect was a racially motivated attack.

Undercurrents, the alternative media service, who reported on the Kent police force's condemnation of the press said: 'The media is a powerful tool to bring positive change but, in the wrong hands, the media can be used to enforce ill founded contempt for entire communities.' Police detectives are currently compiling information on other papers that may need the same caution. ❏
Emily Mitchell

● **In dubious battle** Forget the legality, the morality and even the dubious aims and objectives of the latest US-UK excursion into Iraq. There is a small domestic issue closer home that is concerning UK citizens – most particularly those who voted for the Blair government in May 1997 in the hope of change after 18 years of democratic degradation under Tory government.

In anger more than sorrow, substantial numbers of the latter tore up their Labour Party membership cards at 'the cowardice' of a Party that, fearful of acknowledging even a whisper of dissent in an overwhelming bi-partisan majority, would not allow a parliamentary vote following the emergency debate on the war in the Gulf. Censorship is not confined to what we are allowed to know about the conduct of the war, not even to the suppression of our 'right to know' when our country wages war in our name: this small matter is about the denial of democratic rights in the elected assembly of the UK. ❏
JVH

VALERIE CECCHERINI

Rape and the Prophet

The women of Pakistan have most to fear from their government's attempts to make sharia law supreme

A woman is raped every three hours in Pakistan. Sixty-five per cent of them are under age and one in four is the victim of a group rape. And according to Hina Jilani, a lawyer working for women's rights, that is not the worst of it: 'If a woman is raped but has no evidence to prove it, the very fact that she had admitted to the sexual act may lead to her own prosecution for adultery or fornication – *zina*.

Farida Shaheed, a sociologist and member of *Shirkat Gah*, a Pakistani organisation working to improve the status and rights of women, tells the story of Safia Bibi: 'Eighteen-year-old Safia Bibi was a servant in a wealthy, landed family. She was raped regularly by the man of the house and his son and eventually became pregnant. Her father lodged a suit for rape but, for want of evidence, the court acquitted the rapists and convicted Safia Biba of *zina*. She was sentenced to 15 lashes and three years in prison. We campaigned against the sentence in the national and international media and she was finally acquitted.'

The *zina* ordinance was one of a hotch-potch of laws instituted by its then ruler, General Zia ul-Haq, in his attempt to 'islamise' Pakistan in the 1980s. It covers all extra-marital sexual relations, including rape – which is not itself part of the Quranic definition of the term – and abduction for the sake of sexual assault. The federal *sharia* court acts as the court of appeal for all cases governed by *sharia* law; it is also charged with determining whether the secular laws of Pakistan conform to Islam.

Under the proposed 'islamisation' of the country's legal system now being debated in Pakistan's upper house, the Senate, its jurisdiction would presumably extend to bringing the whole of the country's legal system into conformity with Islamic legal precepts: in other words, it would make Islamic law, complete with all its discriminatory attitudes towards women, supreme.

Fida Mohammed Khan, a judge with the federal sharia court, has no qualms: 'The *zina* ordinance protects the honour of women and their families. For us, women are the jewel of creation; the respect we show them, particularly as mothers, is without equal anywhere. Islam believes fornication and adultery undermines their dignity and, to protect the moral and ethical values of the community as a whole, considers it just and proper to punish those who have offended. Rape is an even more serious offence.'

Chief justice of the *sharia* court Mehboob Ahmed laughed as he expounded the *zina* ordinance: 'I really don't know why this particular law gets people so worked up. With the greatest respect, I think women in western societies are not respected as much as they are in ours. Male chauvinism in the West has seen to it that the law is flexible enough for them to molest women with impunity. But we cannot allow such attitudes to dominate to the detriment of our women; it is precisely the *zina* ordinance that gives them security and freedom.'

Crimes under *zina,* as well as rape, are subject to the law's most severe penalties – *hadd* (literally 'ultimate punishment') – death by stoning or, in the case of an unmarried person, 100 lashes in public. However, Islam is clear that these may only be executed if there is a confession or if four Muslims 'of good standing' have witnessed the crime. While these punishments have never been implemented in Pakistan, the fact that they remain on the statute books acts as a reminder that they still could be. 'They've never been applied because they are totally unacceptable,' stresses Jilani. 'It would be a very unpopular move.' Khan stresses that Islam sees the *hadd* punishments as a last resort to be used as seldom as possible. 'Which is why it has made the conditions of proof so difficult to fulfil. The punishments are there as a deterrent.' The mounting daily toll of rapes gives one leave to doubt their efficacy.

If an accused is found guilty by other proofs, he is liable to the less severe punishments known as *taazir.* These amount to 10 years' imprisonment for violating the *zina* ordinance and from four to 25 years for rape. Until 1996, *taazir* punishments included lashing; this was abolished but, given the rise in gang or group rapes, the *zina* ordinance was amended and the ultimate penalty under *taazir* became capital punishment.

Jilani claims the *zina* ordinance discriminates against women in a number of ways: 'In the first place, to come under the *hadd* penalties, the crime must have been witnessed by four men. The eye-witness statements of women are considered indirect proof – as is the statement of the victim herself. Yet in the majority of rapes, the victim is the only one eye-witness.'

But eye-witnesses must be men, says Khan, 'because the Quran says so. But if a woman inspires belief, then the rapist may be given a *taazir* punishment on her word alone,' he adds.

When an unmarried woman claims to have been raped, the only thing her medical examination proves is that she is no longer a virgin. 'And if she is subsequently unable to prove she has been raped, this fact can be turned against her since the law punishes all sexual relations outside marriage,' explains Jilani. 'The medical examination of the man establishes nothing.' The ordinance discriminates further: women reach their majority – and therefore come under *zina* – at 16 or on reaching puberty, whichever is sooner; men only at 18 or on puberty. 'Children as young as 12 have been punished like adults,' says Jilani. I ask Khan if he thought it right that *zina* made no distinction between physical maturity and mental age. 'There is a clause stipulating that a woman who is mentally disturbed cannot be convicted,' he replies. 'When someone who is too young comes before us, we might be able to discuss whether this clause also allows us to take into consideration the mental age of the accused,' he adds in extenuation.

Unlike the *zina* ordinance, Pakistan's earlier family law, still in operation, considers a woman of age only when she reaches 16. Any form of sexual relation with a minor, even with her husband, is regarded as rape. Now that the *zina* ordinance has brought down the age of responsibility this is no longer the case. 'We want marital rape to be returned to the statutes,' says Samina Rahman, a founding member of the Women's Action Forum. 'Now that this is no longer an offence under the law, no-one takes any notice of it. In a country where many women are married off so young, it's a real problem.'

The Pakistan Commission for Human Rights reckons that only about one in three rapes are reported. 'Even those that are,' says Jilani, 'are not always taken up by the police, and there is seldom a satisfactory outcome. I recently followed the case of a man who raped a 15-year-old girl. The court gave him seven years but, on appeal, the *sharia* court reduced the sentence to two-and-a-half years.'

Rape in Pakistan is traditionally seen as degrading to the woman and the police treat victims with a mixture of contempt and disbelief. 'It's a joke to them,' says Shaheed. 'There are times when they even suspect the victim of crying rape to get at family rivals or their employers. And when you take into account that it's not only the legislators, but all those involved in seeing that the law is carried out as well as the medical officers who do the examinations, it's not surprising that women choose to stay silent.'

A young woman is sitting in Jilani's office. She looks ground-down and at the end of her tether. She tells her story:

'Aided and abetted by a woman, two men from our neighbourhood grabbed me, took me off, beat me and raped me, one after the other. While they were raping and beating me, they took photos. Before letting me go, they told me that if I ever spoke of what had happened, they would kill me, kidnap my daughters and send the photos to the press. My sister-in-law told me not to say anything to my husband: no Pakistani man can accept the idea that this could happen to his wife and she was afraid he would accuse me of having consented to all this and leave me.'

'Some time later, the men who had raped me wanted me to sing for them. They demanded money from me and threatened to show my husband the photos if I didn't give them something. But I have so little money ... Anyway, in the end, my husband found out everything and drove me from the house with the children. I went to stay with my father and we filed a charge of rape against the men. It took eight months before the police even registered the charge. When we went to the police station, the police there were abusive to my father and myself. They were so arrogant. One of them said to me: "You certainly enjoyed yourself with them then!" They treated me like a loose woman. They laughed in my father's face as well and we had to pay 10,000 rupees (cUS$200) just to get the charge registered. When the rapists arrived, they treated them quite differently, offering them a seat and something to drink.'

'Eventually, they arrested one of the men, but he was released with a caution almost immediately. His accomplices, people of means and influence, were never arrested. While they were at the police station, the rapists confessed, but only verbally; afterwards they bribed the police officers with 50,000 rupees (cUS$1,000) to suppress the confession. And the photos are now in the hands of the police: I'm terrified that for another bribe they'd get rid of them as well – the only evidence there is of the crime.'

'A few days ago, a car hit me and I was injured. The drivers said that if I didn't withdraw my charge, the next time would be fatal. The case is still dragging on.'

At this point, she collapses in tears:

'If they're really out to kill me I'd rather commit suicide. But I have to go on: I have my daughters and they are still so small.'

I also met Azra at the same legal advice centre. She had been falsely accused of *zina* several years ago, and spent a month in jail before being released with a caution and, finally, acquitted. Now she told the story of her arrest:

'The officers took me to the police station and locked me in a room. It was during the elections so they were very busy. They forgot all about me and left me there for a day and a night with nothing to eat or drink. I was terribly worried about my children whom I'd had to leave alone at home.

'I'd left a three-year-old daughter and a new-born baby only 15 days old. I had no one to whom I could turn for help. After several months, a friend brought me news of them. In prison, I spoke about the children to one of the guards who told me she could do nothing for me and I must speak to the judge. My 12-year-old daughter was looking after the little ones as best she could. But she was too young to know how to deal with the baby and she died. My three-year-old was later taken into care but by then she was already very ill and died soon after.'

In Pakistani culture, women are seen as the repository of a family's 'honour'. 'If you want to damage a man's honour, you do it through his wife,' explains Jilani. 'In our country, rape is not considered a crime. However, in my opinion, the use of the term "sexual offence" is totally inadequate: rape is a violent crime and has nothing to do with honour. If rape is not treated as a crime, then society will simply continue to treat it as a matter of honour. When a woman has been raped, it's seldom her feelings, the injury to her that is uppermost in the minds of the people around her.'

Women are frequently raped while being held in custody. In 1992, a Human Rights Watch survey showed that 75 per cent of women in prison had been violently assaulted; 62 per cent were the victims of sexual assaults. Today, 47 per cent of all the women in Pakistan's jails are waiting to be tried or sentenced for *zina*. 'It's the most common offence for which people are brought to court,' says Jilani. The majority of the cases are against poor, rural women. Since 1979, when the *zina* ordinance was introduced, thousands of women have been convicted; the majority have eventually been acquitted for lack of proof. But while awaiting a hearing they are imprisoned, often for many months. And even when acquitted and released from jail, they find it hard to return to any sort of normal life.

'Attitudes to these women are appalling,' says Jilani. 'They are seen as women of easy virtue and excluded from society. Their families usually abandon them and it is not unknown for them never to be allowed contact with their children again. They find it hard to get work and some end up as prostitutes. Others seek shelter in the few women's refuges there are in this country. It is next to impossible to rehabilitate them.'

Azra relates what happened to her when she finally got out of prison:
> 'By the time I got out of prison I'd already lost two children, but I found my oldest daughter. Her clothes were in tatters, she was under-nourished and her head was alive with lice ... In my cell, I had often wondered how I was going to face the world, my neighbours and friends once I was out. I wanted the earth to open and swallow me up. When I finally did go back to my place, most people of the people I knew despised me; many avoided me altogether. They thought my honour had been stained. Someone I know helped me to get work, but even today, 13 years later, I still have problems. My daughter is married now, but not long ago, some of her neighbours told her husband about me. He drove her from home and now wants to divorce her.'

Syed Afzal Haider is a lawyer in the supreme court and a member of the Council for Islamic Ideology charged with advising parliament on the extent to which its legislation conforms to Islam. He stressed that what he was about to say was strictly a personal view, one not shared by the majority of the council: 'By definition, a law must have the potential to cover all eventualities. In this respect, I have to say that the *zina* ordinance is seriously defective. But this law has not been passed by parliament; it was imposed by the military dictator General Zia ul-Haq.'

'Our society is deeply religious, but though the religious parties make a great song and dance, they have no intention whatsoever of allowing people to think or make up their own minds. Not a single election in Pakistan has given the religious parties a big enough mandate to form a government. However, no sooner has one or other of the secular parties won power than it consorts with the religious ones. This is a betrayal of its mandate and an insult to the people who put it where it is.'

'All the religious parties supported the military dictatorship and got power that way. They have penetrated the judiciary, the administration, the army and politics. And they have all been used and manipulated by the West, in particular by the USA. The latter has financed and armed them. Even the Taliban benefited from its support. It's a sick game played to the detriment of the interests of the people of this country. Western human rights organisations denounce the current dysfunctional nature of our society, but their analysis seldom looks far below the surface.' ❑

A matter of interpretation

Even the religious community is not of one mind on the *zina* ordinance. In 1981, a number of *ulema* [religious scholars], asked the federal *sharia* court to abolish death by stoning on the grounds that there was no Quranic authority for this. 'However, in the end they refused,' says Fida M Khan. 'Even if it's not actually in the Quran, the Prophet himself ordered it to be carried out.'

Syed Afzal Haider sees things differently. 'This ordinance does not conform to the basis tenets of Islam, that is to say the Quran. It has many anomalies and the council should look into it. We should not forget that there is a great difference between the Quran itself and the many 'interpretations' of it. While the text itself is unchanging, interpretations shift constantly depending on when they are made, the state of society at the time and so on. The Pakistani constitution stipulates that our laws must conform to the Quran and *sunna* (islamic traditions). But in my view, we should develop a new body of laws, one that also takes into account the prevailing attitudes of the present. Today, the accent is on human rights, the search for peace, the development of the potential of all peoples and brotherhood. Nations and peoples are in search of mutual understanding. We must interpret the 'Revelation' in the spirit of our own age and in keeping with internationally accepted principles as outlined in the United Nations Charter, the Universal Declaration of Human Rights and so on. Interpretations from the past may guide us, but they are not the last word on anything. We can discuss these things with people from all over the world and take advantage of other views: no single principle or ideology is adequate for the development of the whole of humanity.'

Khan, on the other hand, considers the *zina* ordinance perfectly adapted to contemporary needs. 'The laws laid down by Allah apply for all time because they relate to fundamental human nature. Men's basic needs and desires do not change though their society may: there will always be murderers and thieves. Allah's laws were good enough for Mohammed's time and so they are today.'

In the course of its campaign against the *zina* ordinance, the Women's Action Forum has canvassed the views of religious leaders who also oppose it. 'This law has nothing to do with the spirit of the Quran,' explains Samina Rahman. 'In the first place, the Quran and *sunna* say that no punishments should be inflicted where social inequalities prevail. We have analysed the ordinance clause by clause exposing the discrepancies between it and the Quran. For instance, if the Quran says that *hadd* punishments can only be inflicted if four Muslims of good standing witness the act, this is tantamount to saying the the individuals concerned should be given the benefit of doubt. Nor does the Quran mention rape; linking rape to *zina* is unquranic and unislamic. A feminist interpretation of the Quran to this effect by a female theologian has been printed in one of our dailies.' ❏

Valérie Ceccherini is a freelance journalist based in France

SARAH KEE

Speak memory

Justice for the victims of Guatemala's dirty war has been slow in coming. Now there are signs of hope

On 9 November 1998, in the Guatemalan town of Salama, history was in the making. The first massacre case from the early-1980s, when some 40,000 people were killed in 'counter-insurgency' operations, had finally arrived in court.

On the street outside, a few banners called for justice and an end to impunity. Inside sat the three defendants – Fermin Lajuj Xitimal, Pablo Gonzalez Gomez and Carlos Chen Gomez – ex-members of the Civil Defence Patrol. The charges stemmed from a massacre in the highland village of Rio Negro on 13 March 1982 when 77 women·and 107 children were tormented and murdered.

The plaintiff, Jesus Tecu Osorio, had worked painstakingly with other survivors and relatives of the dead to push the case forward in the criminal courts. He lost his mother, sister and younger brother in the massacre and is one of the few remaining eye witnesses. Jesus was 10 and vividly remembers the events of that day. Along with other children and their mothers, he was marched up a hill by a group of some 45 patrollers and soldiers. The patrollers, including the three defendants, came from the nearby town of Xococ. Carlos Chen Gomez was in command.

The men kicked and rifle-butted the villagers as they were forced stumbling up the hill. At the top, the patrollers separated some younger women whom they raped repeatedly and then strangled, shot or hacked to death. Jesus watched as his sister was led away. He grabbed his baby brother on the instructions of his mother, the last words he heard her say.

One patroller told Jesus he was going to take him back to Xococ to work for him. He then noticed Jesus' little brother and said: 'But he can't come, he's too small.' Jesus pleaded as the man prepared his machete, turned Jesus round and sliced the small child in two. The patroller was Pedro Gonzalez Gomez, a small, pudgy man in the dock staring fixedly at the floor. When the patrollers finished raping and killing the 177 women and children, Jesus was taken back to Xococ where he worked as a virtual slave for two years until his escape with the help of an elder sister.

Jesus Tecu Osorio was the first witness to give testimony. He chose to speak in Spanish, the language of the court, rather than Maya Achi, his first language. He broke down as he recalled his younger brother's death. Juan Chen Osorio was one of the last. Dates and names were fired at him to find a loophole in his account. The three defendants said they were nowhere near the scene of the crime. They were 'planting trees' and were neither members, nor had any knowledge of the civil patrols.

Through an Achi translator, Juan gave his own version of events. 'The patrollers pushed me to the ground with some of the other children and we were told to stay there and keep our heads faced down. I tried to look up and saw my mother and sister in line with the other women. One by one they disappeared from sight over the brow of a hill and I could hear their screams. I could see my sister and my mother nearing that brow. I was kicked and told to keep my head down. When I looked up again, over to the line of women, my mother and sister were no longer there.' Juan, like Jesus, was held captive by a patroller for two years. As he walked from the witness stand, he fainted.

The trial ended on 30 November; the three ex-patrollers were found guilty of murder and sentenced to death, an outcome which sets an important legal precedent. There are many other massacre cases dating back to the early 1980s, some caught in the inefficiency of the legal system, others not yet presented. Justice, for the first time, dented the impunity that has hitherto surrounded the trauma of that era.

That day, most Guatemalan papers led with the story. But the result does not provide a simple solution to the massive killing of the past. Carlos Chen Gomez, Pedro Gonzalez Gomez and Fermin Lajuj Xitimul were found guilty but the context of their crimes was created by the Guatemalan army. Civil patrollers come low in the hierarchy, so low perhaps that their lives are expendable to protect the instigators who remain in positions of authority to this day.

The civil patrols were set up as local militias with a permanent presence in the communities. From 1982-1983, some 80 per cent of the male population in indigenous zones were integrated into them.

Participation was obligatory: men were ordered to kill their neighbours – or face a brutal fate themselves.

Some Rio Negro witnesses had been threatened with death in the months leading up to the case. The intimidators are well known to the local population; ex-members of the Xococ civil patrol or army informants, all of whom still utilise the protection afforded them by the army. As throughout much of Guatemala, the Rio Negro massacre survivors live side by side with the killers of their loved ones.

In 1996, an official peace accord was signed in Guatemala between the government and the guerrillas of the *Unidad Revoluçionaria Naçional de Guatemala*. Some see it as no more than an élite-brokered agreement, which leaves the civilian population, which suffered the worst effects of the war, to fend for itself.

There have been unofficial attempts to address these effects. The Catholic Church's report *Recuperation of Historical Memory* uses moral, rather than legal, authority to give victims and victimisers a chance to tell their story. Bishop Gerardi, co-ordinator of the project, was murdered in April 1998, 48 hours after the report was made public. The report claimed that the army was responsible for 90 per cent of the 150,000 deaths during the 30-year civil war. It is widely believed that military personnel engineered the death of the bishop. ❏

Sarah Kee is a freelance journalist working in Central America

ELIZABETH ALLARD

Our men in Mexico

Since moving into markets recently left open by the Colombian drug cartels, Mexican traffickers have increased pressure on their country's press. In states bordering the USA they have become particularly powerful.

Mexico, which recently buried three murdered journalists, is in the process of 'Colombianisation': journalists working on drug-related stories know someone, somewhere, is watching them closely.

In early November 1998, television and radio reporter Pedro Valle Hernández was assassinated in the southern state of Guerrero after investigating a local child prostitution ring. A week before, Claudio Cortés García, head of design at *La Crisis* magazine and the local edition of *Le Monde Diplomatique*, was found strangled in his car in Mexico City. Two days before, Fernanado Martínez Ochoa, reporter and spokesman for the secretary of social development in the city of Chihuahua, was also found dead in his car. He had been killed with an axe.

These deaths highlight a rising tide of violence towards the press that has escalated sharply in the last 10 years. Most of the 25 journalists killed since 1970 died after 1988; hundreds more have been victims of threats and violence. Corrupt public officials, law enforcement officers and, more recently, drug traffickers disgruntled by investigations into their business affairs have been implicated in virtually every incident. Most murders remain unsolved: public officials and law enforcement officers consistently hamper and obstruct investigations. The 1991 murder of doctor and columnist Víctor Manuel Oropeza Contreras, stabbed to death by four men in his examining room in Ciudad Juarez after his column in the *Diario de Juarez* alleged a 'close relationship' between the police and drug traffickers, and accused a number of officers of human rights abuses, is a case in point. His case remains open; there have been no convictions and there are no suspects.

In August and September 1997, reporters working for *Reforma*, one of Mexico City's most critical dailies, were abducted and beaten by their assailants, believed to be police officers. David Vicenteño was investigating the disappearance of a police officer who allegedly posed as a double for the drug baron Amado Carillo Fuentes, now dead; David Lizárraga was investigating the shipment of cocaine in an aeroplane owned by the Attorney General's office.

Martínez' death in Ciudad Chihuahua was the latest in a string of attacks on journalists in the north, where one of the most infamous assassinations took place in 1988. Shot while driving to work, Héctor Félix ('The Cat') Miranda died instantly. His column, 'A Little of Something' in the weekly *Zeta* he co-founded in Tijuana, was popular for its tough stance on corruption and drugs. Although two men were convicted for the shooting, the ringleaders have so far escaped justice.

Ironically, the dramatic rise in the number of murders coincides with efforts to open up the one-party political system. His poor handling of the economy, corruption within state-run agencies and election fraud forced President Carlos Salinas de Gortari and his successor Ernesto Zedillo Ponce de Leon to undertake a series of reforms designed to make the ruling PRI (Institutional Revolutionary Party) more accountable. Initial attempts at democratisation and liberalisation did not leave the media untouched. In his 1994 inaugural address, Zedillo identified democratic expression with the freedom of the press.

Despite Zedillo's public statements, an air of ambivalence continues to hang over the role that the press should play in political life. Used to the PRI's informal but effective control, both state and private media outlets have found it difficult to adjust to the changes. News organisations have traditionally paid journalists poorly, on the understanding that the *embutes* – bribes – from government agencies and private companies topped up reporters' salaries. These practices are still common throughout the political establishment: under both Salinas and Zedillo the president's office has offered journalists a wide range of incentives to cover their activities in a favourable light.

Expectations that the press should function as a mouthpiece for the PRI and gloss over instances of corruption persist. In Guaymas, Sonora, the newspaper *La Voz de Puerto* was taken over by officials, including the father of the municipal president, Sara Valle Dessen. The move stemmed from Valle's anger at allegations made about her administration.

Legislative measures to protect freedom of the press have been fraught with contradiction. In April 1998, congressmen introduced a bill prohibiting the reporting by journalists of 'confidential matters' that might occur in the legislature. Days later the same congressmen postponed debating a proposed Law of Social Communication for a year, because they feared that attempts to regulate the press would restrict its freedom. In October, public pressure put discussion of the bill off indefinitely, as controversy raged over several key issues, including regulation of the right to information and the creation of a commission to monitor written and electronic media. Zedillo says he is against the proposed law and favours self-regulation. However, as the murders of Valle, Cortés and Martínez show, while the debate continues, the lack of resolution has created a gap in which violence continues to thrive. ❏

Elizabeth Allard *is studying for a doctorate in Latin American history*

FRANK KERMODE

All into the dark

The announcement that the Oxford University Press has decided to abolish its poetry list has been greeted with cries of disapproval and astonishment

As well as contributing to the reputation of the Oxford University Press, it had been supposed that a measure of support for 50 or so living poets – including Craig Raine, DJ Enright, Peter Porter, Jo Shaphcott – and a few thousand readers was a service well worth its small cost. It is true that OUP would have been celebrated even if it had not published new poetry – Cambridge University Press, no less distinguished, has published none since the eighteenth century – but the poetry list was there and much admired; its withdrawal, so widely deplored, can only be seen as damaging. One must suppose that those who took the decision were well aware of the risk, and found powerful reasons to take it.

From statements to the press it appears that these reason are purely financial. According to Andrew Potter, speaking to the *Guardian* for OUP, 'There's no point in doing it [publishing new verse] unless it's going to allow a reasonable dividend to go back to the original owners, who are the university.' It's hard to believe that until recently anybody can seriously have expected the publishing of new poetry to make lots of money, or that the university would have insisted that it should, yet the Delegacy, the governing body of the Press, is a committee of dons, a university committee, which must, presumably, have approved this decision of its officers. It is rumoured that last year the Press handed over £20 (US$30) million to the university.

If figures provided by the *Guardian* (1 December) are reliable, the annual turnover of the poetry list was £28,000 (US$42,000) – a leader on 2 December thought it might be as much as £50,000 (the Press isn't saying) – and that of the whole company, which is of course a worldwide operation, some £300m. In relation to that budget you might say that the poetry list was costing next to nothing. No doubt the accountants wouldn't have been satisfied even if it could be shown to be nothing; if it made no profit, or a profit too small to satisfy the 'original owners', it obviously must be axed. DJ Enright, a senior Oxford poet, describes this attitude as a 'childish enthusiasm for the bottom line', which may be described as too gentle a way of putting it.

It may not be generally known that OUP is a registered charity. It achieved that status some 20 years ago, when Cambridge University Press managed,with much effort, to win its case with the Charity Commissioners; whereupon OUP slipped in through the opened door. Consequently, the Press, unlike its competitors, is exempt from taxation. This large privilege was granted because CUP managed to convince the authorities that its activities were beneficial to the public and the general culture.

Of course, the grant of charity status doesn't mean these presses are wrong to make a profit; for one thing, they need to be solvent because they cannot be sure the universities would bail them out if things were to go wrong. But the Oxford poetry list, in the opinion of most interested parties manifestly beneficial to the culture, might well have looked like an impressive part of the argument for charitable status. To drop it in order to save a few pennies and some small effort certainly looks very uncharitable. But the Delegates accepted as overruling such considerations the expectation of the university that the Press should 'operate on commercial grounds, especially in this day and age' (*The Times*, 21 November).

The dismay of poets and the interested public is understandable. I'm not sure, however, that they should be as surprised as they seem to be. The present condition of the serious book is such that one more symptom of decline can hardly be astonishing. The bookshops on which we have for so long depended are headed downmarket, no doubt to improve the bottom line. The backlists of the great academic publishers are much shrunk.

A couple of years ago, I lost a large number of books in an accident. Among them were a number of the fine Clarendon Press editions of sixteenth and seventeenth century poets, and these I was particularly anxious to replace. There was a time when if you asked for one of these volumes at Blackwells you would probably walk away with it; but if it was temporarily unavailable, they would ask the Press to bind a copy and you would have it in a couple of weeks. This practice was presumably abandoned when some accountant expressed horror at its cost in warehousing and labour. But it certainly did nothing to shake the customer's confidence in the bookseller and the publisher. Now he or she must trawl the second-hand market. A letter from Janet Montefiori in the *Times Literary Supplement* (27 November) remarks that since living poets are to be excluded from the Press's concerns, 'only dead ones need apply'. But even that isn't true; poets dead as well as alive must suffer the tyranny of the bottom line.

Moreover, everybody who takes an interest in the trade knows how the university presses have pretty well led the way to higher and higher prices: the hardback out of the reach of all but the keenest professional, the paperback, if there is one, about the price you'd expect to pay for a hardback. It is true that all publishers have had to learn to care more about making a profit, and that their promotional habits have changed accordingly. And it is also true that the university presses, despite their advantage of charitable status, have to live in or near this market. But to kill off poetry for the sake of a trifling saving can surely be seen by all except the accountants as an unnecessary and self-destructive act, with negative promotional value. And the learned Delegates, the accountants' bosses, should have been the first to see that. ❏

Frank Kermode was a Cambridge University Press Syndic from 1974-82. He is the author of many books and is currently writing on Shakespeare

BOOKS ON BRAZIL
from the Latin America Bureau

BENEDITA DA SILVA
An Afro-Brazilian Woman's Story of Politics and Love

The extraordinary life story of a remarkable woman. Benedita da Silva is the first black woman to be elected to Brazil's Senate, where 90% of senators are white males. Growing up in extreme poverty - in a family of 15 - in the *favelas* of Rio where she still lives, Bendita has become one of Brazil's most popular political figures.

£10.99 1998 212 pages, photos ISBN 1 899365 21 4 pbk Published in the USA by Food First Books

BRAZIL IN FOCUS
A Guide to the People, Politics and Culture
Jan Rocha

Covers history, people, politics, economy, the Amazon and the environment, and culture. Illustrated throughout with colour and black and white photos. Key facts and figures section, fold-out map, and 'where to go, what to see' section.

£5.99 1997 88pages ISBN 1 899365 00 pbk   Published in the USA by Interlink

WOMEN IN BRAZIL
Caipora Women's Group

This mosaic of articles, poems and interviews paints an evocative picture of life for women in Brazil's shanty towns and peasant villages. Examines the discrimination imposed by machismo, racism and exploitation in factory and farm, but also the varied ways in which women are fighting back.

£5.99 1993 140pages ISBN 0 90615679 3 pbk   Distributed in the USA by Monthly Review Press

Books by post - please add 10% p&p within the UK, 20% overseas - to Latin America Bureau, 1 Amwell Street, London EC1R 1UL. Tel 0171 278 2829 Fax 0171 278 0165
E-mail clee@lab.org.uk Online bookshop www.lab.org.uk Send for a free books catalogue

The Last Empire

Facade of old cathedral, Macau – Credit: Chris Stowers/Panos

Portugal's 500-year empire comes to an end on 20 December 1999 with the return of Macau to China. *Index* looks at the legacy of 'Lusophonia', the archipelago of language and culture that embraces Portugal, Angola, Mozambique, Guinea-Bissau and East Timor

File compiled by Michael Griffin

Crónica

there were boats and boats that left
making our life out of this matter
tars and soldiers that embarked
and folks who cried at the farewell

we were always or almost or close to
running after uncertain shadows
always dreaming of indias and brazils
and discovering our very own misadventures

memory of coral reddened
by blood and suffering mixed
if it rips darkness and storms
brings us also entangled in seaweed

and won some lost some sailing
through cruel fortune and sudden wind
and the time was passing slowly
so slowly in the wheels of fortune

that either we find ourselves or
we are drifting once again
in this corner that is our very own floor
without even our song surviving us

Vasco Graça Moura *is a Portuguese essayist, poet and novelist.* Crónica *is included in* Letras do Fado Vulgar, *(Quetzal, 1997)*

ANA DUARTE MELO

The last Empire

A common language is the surviving memorial to the the wreck of the world's oldest – and last – European empire

When the final fragment of Portugal's 500-year empire, Macau, reverts to Chinese rule on 19 December 1990, the colony's change of sovereignty is unlikely to attract the same spectacular level of attention as Britain's handover of Hong Kong in June 1997. Yet, it in one way at least, it is a more significant historic milestone. After 442 years of continuous occupation, Portugal will become the last European colonial power to withdraw from Asia.

It is a purely symbolic end of era. 'Portugal outside Portugal' – the term used by the dictator António de Oliveria Salazar to define the complex agglomeration of empire – had been whittled down from an area 22 times the size of the 'fatherland' to Macau's mere 16skm 25 years ago when a mutiny by middle-ranking military officers in Lisbon blossomed overnight into a fully-fledged Marxist revolution.

No empire stands above reproach and the Portuguese one far less than most, for it thrived, for all but a few decades of its duration, upon the extensive strip-mining of African manpower to labour in the sugar plantations of Brazil, which only formally abolished slavery in 1888 and has still to address the consequences. In Angola, Mozambique and Guinea-Bissau, jettisoned in mid-war one year after the revolution of 25 April 1974, thousands of fleeing settlers exacerbated decades of exploitation by destroying or vandalising everything they could not take to Portugal. East Timor, always last in Portuguese priorities, was abandoned to its fate. Lisbon left its colonies with the most threadbare of social, economic and institutional infrastructures from which to weave some kind of independent existence.

But that is not the final epitaph on the Portuguese empire. 'Portugal outside Portugal' has evolved into a cultural and cross-racial inheritance, binding together linguistic enclaves in Europe, Africa, Asia and Latin America in a geographical template that recalls the currents followed by the early navigators – and the slaves. *Fado*, Portuguese blues, and *saudade*, the spirit of futile yearning that infects it, are everyday currency among 140 million Portuguese-speaking Brazilians, as well as in Angola, Mozambique, Guinea-Bissau, Cape Verde and São Tomé and Principe where Portuguese remains the official language.

Cape Verde, São Tomé and Principe, Luanda, Ilha de Moçambique and Goa were originally founded as supply points on the maritime route to spice-rich Asia, while the mid-Atlantic Azores provided the same service on the voyage to Brazil. They were little more than the fortress-enclaves of merchant-adventurers, situated offshore where possible, which used client chiefs on the mainland as sub-contractors in the slave trade.

Of the 1,832 white settlers in Angola in 1846, 1,466 lived in Luanda and the narrow strips of land they had acquired on the coast. But few came voluntarily and the early colonisation of Africa was almost exclusively carried out by *degregados*, convicted criminals with no literacy and few skills to impart. The shortage of white women encouraged inter-marriage and led to the empowerment of a *mestiço* or mixed race class that outnumbered the Portuguese until the accelerated migrations of the mid twentieth century. Creoles oiled the slave trade, the commerce with India and made what few hesitant steps 'Portugal' took into the interior of its loosely-controlled, but extensive, empire. They also contributed to the myth, still current today, that the Portuguese empire, more than any other in the twentieth century, had looked beyond differences of race and class to a higher, more harmonious mingling of origins.

Portugal experienced three imperial phases in its 500 years of empire. The first followed rapidly on Vasco da Gama's return to Lisbon in September 1499, and focused on East Asia, where the proseletysing efforts of the Society of Jesus went hand in hand with commercial profit. The second was based on Brazil from where, in a foretaste of the third and final phase, Portugal was ruled from afar, like a colony of its own colonies, by Dom João VI who took refuge there from Napoleon's invading armies in the early years of the last century. Even after independence in 1822, Brazil remained the preferred destination of

Portuguese settlers, with some 1.3 million making their way there in the 40 years after 1886.

A similar number left for Africa between 1926 and 1966, the period dominated by Salazar's *Estado Novo* dictatorship; another 1.2 million escaped to low-paid jobs in the EU during the 1970s. The stimuli for the third imperial adventure had been provided by the Congress of Berlin in 1884 and the realisation that, with its small and largely rural population, Portugal could not hope to keep up with its European rivals in the post-slavery era without commercialising its neglected African assets. By 1960, there were 177,000 Portuguese in Angola, but their calibre had not improved since the days of the *degredados*: Over half of them had never been to school and most converged on the cities, where they dominated low-paid jobs to the detriment of the *mestiços* and *assimilados.*

After 13 years of nationalist insurrection, on 25 April 1974, war-weary officers of the Armed Forces Movement (MFA) overthrew the regime that had ruled for nearly half a century. As fighting broke out among rival liberation groups and, in November 1975, Cuba dispatched soldiers to support the Marxist *Movimento Popular de Libertaçao de Angola* (MPLA), the Portuguese settlers panicked. They packed their possessions into thousands of wooden crates and departed en masse, 'convinced that in this country there would be no more life and only the cemeteries would remain'. ❏

Ana Duarte Melo grew up in Mozambique, worked as a journalist in Macau TV for four years and now teaches at Oporto's School of Art and Design

ANTONIO DE FIGUEIREDO

The shallow grave of empire

Secrecy was the cornerstone of empire, a *masque* that distorted both the ruler and the ruled

In 1974, Portugal held not only the remnants of the oldest overseas empire in history but the longest record of censorship in the western world. The two facts were interrelated. The centuries-old regime of censorship had the double effect of isolating the monolinguistic Portuguese from the outside world, while secluding their far-flung colonies in Africa and Asia from inquisitive international observers. There was tacit collusion in this strategy at an international level. Having won World War II, the UK and the USA provided diplomatic cover for the abuses of the Salazar régime, which they turned into a cornerstone of NATO in 1949, when the expediencies of the Cold War began to overrule moral scruples. Surrounded by Franco's Spain – to which Salazar was allied through the Iberian Pact – and the beckoning sea, and with its overseas colonies marooned in a kind of linguistic autism, the *Estado Novo* dictatorship seemed unassailable on Europe's westernmost edge.

With its empire transformed into a unitary state by dictatorial decree, the Portuguese, conditioned to feeling threatened by Spain, but themselves oppressed, turned into the oppressors of others. Portugal's half millennium of colonialism had been based primarily on slavery, which had stocked Brazil and its plantations with some 3.5 million kidnapped Africans. The empire's most negative feature would remain the exploitation of Africans as tools for the production of cash crops, and sometimes as an export in themselves – in the case of Mozambique, to work the mines of South Africa. The relations between empire and censorship and, in turn, censorship and slavery, formed part of a hidden history which had to be told if both Portuguese and Africans were to disentangle themselves from the quagmire into which they had fallen.

In 1974, the world's attention was focused on Vietnam and the proposed impeachment of President Richard Nixon. Portugal was in the throes of an oil boycott for having allowed the USA use of its air base in the Azores during the 1973 Arab-Israel war. Many still think that the coup's ideologues took advantage of the opportunity provided by such distractions in US politics to make their own move on power. Be that as it may, the day after the April *putsch* Salazar's successor, Professor Marcelo Caetano, quietly surrendered and a youthful Armed Forces Movement emerged. It had little or no connection with either the existing civil opposition or the clandestine Communist Party led from abroad. Determined to proceed with a withdrawal from the war-torn empire, over the next 18 months the officers leading the coup briefly placed Portugal in the vanguard of revolutionary idealism in Europe – the famous 'Carnation Revolution'.

Overnight, political exiles like myself had all become historians. Journalists and diplomats in Lisbon could only speculate as to the likely repercussions of the coup in Spain, where the Franco regime was sapped by the advanced age of the dictator, or for NATO, of which Portugal had been a founder member. But the ripples spread further, notably in southern Africa, where Mozambique and oil-rich Angola are strategically situated, and in Guinea-Bissau, where a model revolutionary army was well on the way to military victory. It was felt in the forgotten outposts of Macau and East Timor, then still independent of Indonesia's heavy-handed rule.

Portugal being a poor country, with a long entangled history, most reporters did not care to delve into the complicated historical and political background. 'Dictatorship fatigue' at home, and 'war fatigue' on three distant colonial fronts in west and southern Africa were immediate enough reasons for a revolutionary turn of events which, with hindsight, seemed only too predictable. But it was the suddenness of the collapse of an old, allied regime that surprised everyone – even those involved in the coup. But for a few specialised historians – and even some leading African nationalists – the confusingly simplistic explanation was regarded as the ultimate 'achievement' of Portugal's long centuries of autocratic rule and nearly 50 years of the Salazar/Caetano regime.

One of the most memorable essays on the cultural impact of this prolonged experience of censorship was written by novelist José Cardoso Pires, while visiting professor at King's College London and published as 'Changing a Nation's Way of Thinking' in *Index on Censorship* in 1972, two years before the coup. He begins:

'In the five centuries of its publishing history, Portugal has experienced 420 years of censorship. In statistical terms, therefore, publishing in Portugal is a cultural activity which has been carried out at a 'rate of repression' of 84 per cent. For generation after generation, while political regimes and scientific and cultural movements have succeeded one another, a slow procession of martyrs has found its way along the thousands of miles which would be covered by the texts thrown onto bonfires and relegated to dusty archives. Resistance has become historical reality, constantly renewed by the subterfuges devised to evade the watchful eyes of the authorities. And the tradition of repression has been increasingly refined, culminating in the clearly-defined technical unity which it achieved under the Salazar dictatorship.'

Pires arrived at his total by adding the singularly long duration of the Inquisition in Portugal – from 1536 to 1821 – to that of the *Estado Novo* which, at the time of writing, had been in power for 46 years. The balance was made up by keying in the short-lived liberal and parliamentary systems under the constitutional monarchy and the 18-year-long First Republic (1910-28), but these periods were only intermittent exceptions to a continuum of persistent repressive rule. Portugal's experience of censorship cannot be blamed exclusively on the Inquisition and other Catholic-influenced traditions that kept the country for ever on the fringe of the French and Industrial revolutions and, under Salazar, secluded it from the mainstream of accelerated evolution in a crucial half-century of change. Other Catholic states, like France and Italy, gave birth to the Renaissance and the Enlightenment, and Ireland enjoyed a remarkable record of anti-colonial resistance.

Its roots can be more confidently traced to the cloud of secrecy that enveloped the era of maritime exploration and empire building in the fifteenth and sixteenth centuries. To this day, historical researchers of the Discoveries, as well as empire-building and the long period of slavery, complain that Portuguese kings exercised censorship over all records that might reveal secrets likely to harm Portuguese trade. By over-extending its geographic frontiers, Portugal became the captive of an empire which it had no military means to defend without the protection of the 600-year-old Anglo-Portuguese alliance. Censorship, as a consequence, evolved into a frontline strategy to ward off threats from existing or potential imperial rivals, the protests of the nineteenth century abolitionists and, in the early 1960s, apologists for British, French, Dutch and Belgian decolonisation. A linguistic reminder of both the weight of British influence and Lisbon's attempts to hide its activities survives in the fact that *para Ingler ver* – 'for the English to see' –is the idiomatic equivalent of 'keeping up appearances' throughout Lusophone Africa.

The censor's blue pencils and rubber stamps became the main instruments of cultural control within the empire. The guidelines, issued by the *Estado Novo* to the General Directive Board of Censorship Services to the Press in August 1931, remained basically unchanged throughout the subsequent decades and were deceptively simple and wide. 'The Press,' read clause 16, 'has the main role of keeping minds calm, forgetting all hatred and passions, mobilising the efforts of all Portuguese towards the good of the Nation.' Under the Constitution, the advocacy of decolonisation was high treason, punishable by detention and, eventually, sentences of up to 24 years in prison.

In the 'overseas provinces', additional censorship orders were published which were publicly unknown in Portugal because the censors never allowed their publication in the press. One was intended to curb the denunciations of forced labour in Angola and Mozambique that, from time to time, were published abroad by travellers, notably Nevinson and Ross. One had appeared as a clause in the 'Labour Code of the Natives of Portuguese Colonies', published in 1928, little more than two years after the emergence of the *Estado Novo*: 'All Portuguese, as well as all individuals of other nationalities residing in Portuguese territory, who intentionally in public speeches, manifestos, books, booklets, newspapers or other periodicals to be sold or distributed free of payment to the public, propagate false information aiming at showing the existence of slavery or the traffic of slaves within the Portuguese colonies, will be punished with fines from Escudo 20,000, or up to two years imprisonment, and may still be liable to expulsion from Portuguese territory.'

Not even dissidents within the regime like Henrique Galvão, a former administrator in Angola, were spared the fury of these draconian laws. As a deputy in the National Assembly and general inspector to the colonies, Galvão, in principle, was entitled to immunity. But in 1947, he presented a report of a recent tour in which, after listing a wide range of abuses, he concluded that 'only the dead were exempt from forced labour'; slaves, he implied, were not owned individually, as in old days, but collectively by the state. He was forced into retirement and, after a period of harassment by PIDE [Policia Internacional de Defasa do Estado] was eventually tried for high treason in 1952. Seven years later he escaped from hospital and took refuge in the Argentine embassy, from where he went to South America in 1959. In the same year, he orchestrated the hijack of the luxury liner *Santa Maria*, sailing her to Angola on the maiden voyage of a trend of violence that has endured until the present. When the worldwide publicity made it impossible for the censors to keep the event out of the Portuguese press, editors were told to reduce coverage to a minimum — and always to refer to it in editorials as a 'vicious, political act'.

The regime's methods were more dramatically epitomised by the case of the rebel leader of the National Independence Movement, General Humberto Delgado. Upon arrival in exile in Rio de Janeiro, he found it impossible to make statements about the empire for they would incriminate, by proxy, his supporters in Portugal. On Algerian independence, he moved to Algiers to be closer to the leaders of the African liberation movements. He exhorted the armed forces to 'use their courage' to overthrow the regime, rather than fight black nationalists in the hundred-mile long fronts in Guinea-Bissau, Angola and Mozambique. Lured by PIDE into a meeting near Badajoz, just across the Spanish border, he was 'disappeared' on 12 February 1965.

His, and the body of his Brazilian secretary, were found two months later in a shallow grave in Villanueva del Fresno. What followed had the significance that goes with political legends. He was buried three times in haste. First by PIDE, which dumped the bodies in Villanueva del Fresno; then by the Spanish authorities, who deposited the remains in the local cemetery where they remained throughout the colonial wars which he had stridently warned were repugnant and unwinnable. Even after Salazar's death, his corpse was refused entry into Portugal. The family waited until the April revolution, but a new development intervened. Fearing criticism for their belated coup after 13 years of colonial torment, the Armed Forces Movement decided that Delgado's remains should be buried quietly in a Lisbon cemetery within hours of arrival. It took 25 years for his bones to be deposited in the National Pantheon.

From London, and in twice weekly broadcasts to Portugal and the African 'provinces' on the BBC Portuguese service, I covered the freedom fight until 1974. Since then I have travelled assiduously to Portugal and Southern Africa following developments since decolonisation. For me, that process was more important for the birth of five new African nations than the end of an ancient empire. Reaching the age when one is more given to doubts than certainties, of two facts I am sure: one, that the newly independent African nations will, after an initial period, gradually find their own way in the international community; and two, that Portugal, without its empire, no longer needs hidden history or secretive diplomacy.

As for the end of the empire, there can be no better epitaph than that of the British historian, JH Plumb, in his introduction to Charles Boxer's classic *The Portuguese Seaborne Empire*:

> 'At a terrible cost Portugal opened the doors to a wider world, one that she could neither dominate nor control; with history's usual malice she was quickly overtaken and left moribund, a pensioner in the world stakes; possessing enough for survival, too little for glory. And like the aged, she still clung desperately and meanly to all that she possessed hoping to outlive the times – an unlikely prospect. And yet indelibly her name is written across the world's history; an extraordinary achievement for so small, so poor a country.' ❑

Antonio de Figueiredo *is the author of* Portugal: 50 years of Dictatorship *(Penguin) and, after 38 years with the BBC World Service, its longest-serving outside contributor*

ZECA AFONSO

Grândola

Grey town of Grândola
Land of brotherhood
The people call the shots
Within you, O city walls

Within you, O city walls
The people call the shots
Land of brotherhood
Grey town of Grândola

A friend in every corner
Equality in every face
Grey town of Grândola
Land of brotherhood

Land of brotherhood
Grey town of Grândola
Equality in every face
The people call the shots

In the shadow of an oak tree
I forgot how old it was
I swore to take as my companion
Your will, Grândola

Grândola, your will
I swore to take as my companion
In the shadow of an old oak tree
I forgot how old it was

The story is an attractive one. Zeca Afonso's *Grândola* was the song that, half an hour into 25 April 1974, gave the signal for the military coup. The song was a *fado*, meaning 'destiny', the song-form definitive of Lisbon's popular culture. Zeca Afonso was one of a generation of *fadistas* who, from the 1960s onwards, tried to reclaim *fado* from Salazar's licensed '*fado* houses' and return it to the streets of its origin. With its rousing but haunting tune, *Grândola* was the right song for a revolution.

The facts are more prosaic. That night, there were two signals. The first, broadcast on military radio within the Lisbon infantry barracks, announced the time as 'five to eleven' and then played *Depois de Adeus* (After Saying Goodbye) by Paulo de Darvalhos which, two weeks earlier, had been Portugal's entry for the Eurovision song contest in Brighton. Then at 0.30, a newscaster on Radio Clube Portugues (RCP), read aloud the opening strophe of *Grândola*. No music, just the metaphor. Three hours later, both the RCP and the televison station were in the hands of the revolutionaries and the government was without the means to mobilise its own forces.

In the weeks that followed, the whole of Portugal seemed to be singing *Grândola*. Today, with new words and accompanied by idealised village scenes, it is used on television to market a brand of olive oil. ❏

Landeg White

LANDEG WHITE

Empire's revenge

The traumas of decolonisation were not felt in the colonies alone – Portugal itself is still living through the aftershocks of 1974

'By the early 1970s,' wrote Robert Harvey of the *Economist* 'it had become obvious that Portugal had not so much succeeded in leaving its mark on Africa as Africa succeeded in leaving its mark on Portugal.'

Africa was at the very heart of the 'Carnation Revolution' of April 1974. Facing defeat in Guinea-Bissau, and unwilling to be blamed (as their seniors had been for the loss of Goa in 1961), captains in the Portuguese army mutinied. The long tradition of army intervention in politics through coups and *pronunciamentos* made it credible to call the mutiny a revolution. Its leaders, who six months earlier had been prosecuting the fascist regime's African wars, declared themselves Marxists, converted by the propaganda of those they had been fighting.

But what was to be done about the empire? Portugal's love-hate affair with Africa did not begin with the European Scramble of 1890. It dates from 711, when a Berber army from Morocco invaded the Iberian peninsula. Until the middle of the thirteenth century, much of what now constitutes Portugal was ruled by 'Moors' as a semi-independent outpost of Islam, leaving an indelible mark on both landscape and culture. After the 're-conquest', the first Portuguese voyages down Africa's Atlantic coast were driven by the wish to secure the nation by taking the 'Moors' in the rear.

When these voyages began to yield riches, from gold and slaves and the spice trade, an economy grew which became dangerously dependent on the exploitation of overseas resources and, later, on remittances from Portuguese emigrants. In the process, a new motive for colonisation

MFA
SENTINELA DO POVO

DINAMIZAÇÃO CULTURAL • ACÇÃO CÍVICA

emerged: Portugal's commercial and political rivalry with Spain. By 1974, it had been argued for three centuries that without the status conferred by its overseas possessions, Portugal risked forfeiting its very identity. Without Empire, it was just another Catalonia.

The loss of Africa, therefore, was far more painful than anything experienced by Britain. Portuguese colonists were not Oxbridge-trained administrators with their children at English public schools and retirement homes waiting in the Home Counties. They were peasants from Alto Minho and Tras-os-Montes, with nowhere to go but the impoverished villages they had originally fled.

The revolutionary leaders in 1974 faced two immediate problems. First, the army on the ground in Africa, much of it by this stage locally recruited, refused to continue fighting. Politicians were left with no option but to put the best face on surrender. Even where the handover was disputed, elections played no part in the process. In Guinea-Bissau, power was swiftly awarded to Luiz Cabral's *Partido Africano para a Independência da Guiné e Cabo Verde*. In Mozambique, the Lusaka Accord of September 1974 delivered the country to Samora Machel's *Frente de Libertação de Moçambique*, with full independence scheduled for June 1975. In Angola, where the financial stakes were highest, Portugal's failure was most pronounced. After a year trying to patch together a coalition government from the rival liberation movements, two separate independence celebrations were organised, one in Luanda handing the country over to Agostinho Neto's *Movimento Popular de Libertação de Angola*, the other in Nova Lisboa (Huambo) handing it to Jonas Savimbi's *União Nacional para a Independência Total de Angola*. Portugal's last act as colonial power was to bequeath to Angola the civil war that has been waged until the present day.

Meanwhile, a second problem loomed. On 24 June 1975, the revolutionary government published a decree-law entitled Preservation of Portuguese Nationality. Among other provisions, it maintained the right to Portuguese citizenship of any man born in the overseas territories while under Portuguese rule, and any woman married to, widowed by or divorced from a man falling into that category, together with their minor children. This astonishing decision, giving the populations of Angola, Mozambique and Guinea-Bissau (not to mention Timor and Macau) the right to remain Portuguese, had its antecedents in Salazar's colonial 'reforms' of 1961. These had granted 'natives' the same legal rights as Portuguese citizens by converting 'colonial territories' into 'overseas provinces' of Portugal.

It was difficult for a revolutionary government in 1974 to revoke such rights. Faced with the army's refusal to fight, the government may have hoped to create in Africa communities whose first loyalty would continue to be to Portugal. Inadvertently, however, the decree-law conferred on whole populations the right to migrate to Portugal.

How many settlers left Africa for Portugal between 1974 and 1976 has never been established. In the run-up to the twin elections of April and June 1976, it was estimated that the true number was 800,000, increasing the population by 10 per cent, doubling the unemployment rate and constituting one third of additions to the electoral register (most of them with right-wing affiliations). An authoritative study published in 1987 and based on the 1981 national census, reduced this estimate to 505,087, but omitted to include two categories of people. First, the inhabitants of shanty towns in Lisbon and Setubal districts who had not been enumerated in 1981. Second, an unknown number who had sound reasons for not responding accurately to a loaded question about where they were living before December 1973. Two conclusions are relevant: that the truer figure is nearer 700,000, and that a substantial number of 'returnees', as many as one quarter of a million, were people of varied ethnic origins who had never before lived in Portugal.

Some of these had been close to the colonial regime and had good reasons for choosing to migrate. But the majority were effectively stateless and paperless, caught up in the turmoil of the times. They were people who boarded emergency refugee flights in Malange, expecting to fly to Luanda, and found themselves disembarking in Lisbon. One former resettlement official remembers 2,000 arriving in a single day, every one of them black. No-one was refused entry and, under the terms of the 1975 decree-law, there were few grounds on which anyone might have been refused.

In Angola and Mozambique, it is insisted all who left were Portuguese (as indeed everyone was under the 1975 decree-law). In Portugal, it is assumed the shanty town dwellers are immigrants from Cape Verde. Many, in a painfully slow process, have been re-housed. There is a magnanimity to be celebrated in this yet tens of thousands remain outside society as the metropolitan victims of the revolution's failure to resolve its African dilemmas.

Portugal celebrates 25 April annually with considerable pomp and circumstance. For some, especially on the left, Africa with its own failed revolutions seems forgotten. On the right, in a reversal of logic, the revolution itself is blamed for the loss of the colonies. Demeaning contrasts are drawn between Britain's measured decolonisation and the counter-scramble of Portugal's exit. There are bizarre histories in which the struggle for democracy in Portugal is located not in the Salazar years but between April 1974 and November 1975 when Otelo de Saraiva Carvalho (in his own account 'a Marxist who had never read Marx') was ousted from the Armed Forces Movement.

A better way of understanding this, and the national trauma involved, is to realise that Portugal has never really given up her colonies. Decolonisation is a process of recognising that the time to depart is overdue and (perhaps) that one should never have been there in the first place. Portugal's departure was more akin to mass deportation, an entirely different psychological experience. It bequeaths the illusion that history has somehow gone

Angola –
Credit: Rex

wrong and requires correction – rather as the Spanish 'occupation' from 1580 to 1640 was inauthentic and not part of the 'national truth'.

For many, empire is still there, on the outer fringes of *saudade*, the national sense of nostalgia which moulds its expectations for the future. How else to comprehend the outrage of a leading People's Party MP at being banned by the Angolan government from negotiating with Jonas Savimbi on Angolan soil? That she was dealing with the leader of an armed uprising against a legitimately elected government of a sovereign state simply never occurred to her. How else to explain the upheaval on the editorial board of an academic journal which published an article reporting, in wholly anodyne terms, Mozambique's English-language policy? How else to understand the foreign ministry's attempt to subvert, rather than welcome, Nelson Mandela's appeal to ex-President Suharto for the release of East Timor leader Xanana Gusmão?

This is very far from being the whole story. As early as the 1960s, Portuguese emigrants from Alto Minho and Tras-os-Montes were abandoning Portugal's African wars and voting with their feet for Europe. In retrospect, these were the precursors of the revolution, defining before it had happened its only possible destination. For them, and especially for their grown-up children, Africa is a distant bewilderment. Returning each August from France, Germany and Britain, they are embarrassed at their country's 'backwardness', as though confirming afresh the old jibe that Africa begins at the Pyrenees.

I have a colleague, seven years old in 1974, whose only memory of the Carnation Revolution is that one week he was being taught French by nuns, the next being taught English by 'communists'. Like Britain, but more cheerfully, Portugal is resigned to Europe. Like Britain, after empire, there is nowhere else to go. But there is a new, rampant racism, very much on the European model, directed against those recent illegal African immigrants who came to build Expo 1998 and the new Ponte Vasco da Gama. Some sleep in cardboard boxes along the Avenida da India. The ironies are painful. They will not go away. ❏

Landeg White has worked in Trinidad, Malawi, Sierra Leone, Zambia and the UK and now teaches at the Universidade Aberta in Lisbon. His verse translation of Camões' epic poem The Lusíads *has just been awarded the Texeira Gomes prize*

HILARY OWEN

Exiled in its own land

'Whores or lesbians – who cares what they call us, so long as the battle is fought and not lost.' (*Novas Cartas Portuguesas*)

Novas Cartas Portuguesas (New Portuguese Letters) was written in 1971 by Maria Isabel Barreno, Maria Teresa Horta and Maria Velho da Costa, all from Lisbon and Marias all three – hence the name by which they became known around the world 'The Three Marias'. When their book first appeared in 1972 it was an instant popular success. It also enraged the censors of the *Estado Novo* dictatorship who prosecuted the three women and their publisher for 'offending public morals' and 'abusing' the freedom of the press. This was an unusually draconian measure even for the times. As Duarte Vidal, Isabel Barreno's defending counsel, pointed out, 'the accusation of pornography and offence of public morals was merely a pretext hiding the real reasons for the criminal prosecution, which were essentially political.'

It was not the first time that a woman writer in Portugal had suffered the absurdity of a patriarchal regime suppressing female eroticism in literature as pornographic. Natália Correia's *Antologia de Poesia Portuguesa Satírica e Erótica* was a famous case in point. What distinguished *Novas Cartas Portuguesas* was the way it exploited collective solidarity in both its literary format and its courtroom strategy. The three co-authors refused to identify the perpetrator of the anonymous passages on which the prosecution case was based.

The theme of *Novas Cartas Portuguesas* drew its inspiration from the seventeenth century French classic, *Lettres Portugaises*, in which a Portuguese nun, Mariana Alcoforado, seduced and abandoned by her French cavalier lover, takes up the pen to bemoan her fate and, in so doing, overcomes it. The Marias used her story to denounce the oppression of women throughout history. The result was a playfully inconclusive, dialectic debate allowing a radical feminist focus on women's sexual self-determination to alternate with Marxist materialist readings of history and protests against Portugal's Colonial Wars in Africa, economic migration and the hegemony of the Catholic Church.

The case drew committed, but limited, support from Portugal's intellectual left. In 1973, an international appeal was addressed via Christiane Rochefort to the French Women's Liberation Movement. The stage was set for international feminist action on an unprecedented scale. The radical feminist Robin Morgan organised a Broadway benefit evening with dramatic presentations from the book. TAP airline offices and Portuguese embassies were picketed. Demonstrations were held across major cities in Europe and the USA. Ruth Escobar led protest actions in Brazil. In London, Helder Macedo brought the case to public attention via *The Times* and the UK solidarity campaign staged a series of readings. Feminists in Paris processed to Notre-Dame bearing effigies of the Three Marias and singing a somewhat revised version of the *Dies Irae*.

The furore caused severe international embarrassment to Caetano's regime which was already discredited for its poor record on human rights. On 25 April 1974, a non-violent Marxist coup overturned the dictatorship and the Three Marias were officially pardoned in May. The euphoria did not last. The diversity of opinion, which had been the strength of *Novas Cartas Portuguesas* in the broad coalition of anti-fascist resistance, rapidly undermined the solidarity between the Three Marias in the schismatic events which followed. The Communists (PCP) and radical left enjoyed a brief and turbulent period at the helm (1974/75) before being progressively ousted by the Socialists and pressured by the militant conservatism of northern Portugal. The PCP failed to mobilise the popular support it had counted on. A counter-coup in November 1975 marked the turning point on the road to Portugal's emergence as a democratic republic in 1976 and the radical Marxist dreams behind the 'Carnation Revolution' lay in ruins.

Shortly after the Three Marias' release, the trio split publicly and acrimoniously when Maria Velho da Costa dissociated herself in the national press from *Novas Cartas Portuguesas* and from radical feminism. She went on to participate in Communist Party anthologies such as

Escrita e Combate and entered the debates over literature and instrumentalism which preoccupied the Portuguese Writers' Association at their 1st Congress in May 1975. Her article 'Revolution and Women', published in *Cravo* ('Carnation') in 1976, locates women's oppression in a Marxist materialist tradition and praises those who took to the streets in 1974.

Teresa Horta and Isabel Barreno went on to become founders of the Portuguese women's liberation movement, or MLM, partly inspired by US models. Its pro-abortion and contraception agenda proved predictably inflammatory in a traditional Catholic culture. The MLM's only public rally, in Lisbon's Parque Eduardo VII in 1974, was physically attacked by male demonstrators and opposed by the larger rival women's organisation, the Women's Democratic Movement (MDM), backed by the PCP. At the 1st Portuguese Writers' Congress in 1975, a delegate named Teresa Crespo called for *Novas Cartas Portuguesas* to be read aloud to illiterate working-class women in the service of the Cultural Revolution rather than, as was increasingly the case, being reconsigned to obscurity for its literary 'élitism'. It was a touchingly isolated cry coming barely 12 months after the campaign to rescue the text from fascist censorship.

Novas Cartas Portuguesas remained available in French, German and English long after the third Portuguese edition in 1980 looked set to be the last. Despite the text's obscurity in Portugal, the memory of the Three Marias case was periodically revived in Europe and America. It was adapted for the stage as *La Clôture* (The Cloister) in the Cité Universitaire Theatre, Paris 1978. The German poet Barbara Köhler pays tribute to the Three Marias in her collection *Cor/responde* (1997). Following the successful reissue of the English translation by Readers International in 1994, the original benefit reading was restaged in the Albert Hall's Little Garden in December 1996, with the same four actresses reprising their roles before an audience which included Maria Isabel Barreno. Although the essentialist concept of a 'universal feminine' is virtually untenable in the multicultural, transnational feminist climate of the 1990s, it is evident that the Three Marias' case continues to inspire, and to afford valuable insights into the complexities of feminist theory and practice in transnational arenas.

During the 1980s, the case was occasionally cited in Portugal as a symbolic watershed for the booming trend in women's writing, but the text itself remained unavailable. Following the lifting of censorship and the 1970s' imperative of 're-learning to write', many Portuguese novelists developed new narrative strategies directed towards a collective coming to terms with its recent history. In this climate all three of the Marias developed successful individual careers as creative writers, whilst pursuing parallel occupations in journalism, editing and teaching, cultural and educational diplomacy and raising their families. They never worked collaboratively with each other again though Teresa Horta, the most high profile radical feminist of the three, continued to commemorate *Novas Cartas Portuguesas* in *Mulheres* magazine which she edited during the 1980s.

Graça Abranches, a leading feminist academic from Coimbra University, once aptly described *Novas Cartas Portuguesas* as a 'text exiled in its own land'. Rereading with 25 years' hindsight Antonio de Figueiredo's review of the case (*Index* 2/1974), I was powerfully struck by his reference to the *Estado Novo*'s euphemistic description of prolonged censorship prosecutions as keeping books 'out of the market'. This ground-breaking text of Portuguese feminist history has effectively remained 'out of the market' in its own country since it last went out of print in 1980.

For various reasons, including the tenacity of feminist academics and the growth of international university networks, Women's Studies has gained a foothold in the higher education system, notably at the Universidade Aberta and at Coimbra University, which now offers 'Estudos Feministas'. The republication of Portugal's out-of-print feminist classics is an urgent priority for programmes such as these and for women's education in general. With the plaudits still resounding for José Saramago, Portugal's first Nobel laureate, a rather less well publicised event in the literary world is also worthy of our celebration. At the end of 1997, after an 18-year silence, a new edition of *Novas Cartas Portuguesas* was published by Dom Quixote. ❑

Hilary Owen *is Lecturer in Portuguese at the University of Manchester*

BARRY LOWE

Out of school

It's almost a year before Macau returns to China in December 1999, but some people are already having a foretaste of what that may mean. After four hundred often turbulent years in China, it could be the Jesuits' last stand

An elderly man in command of a US$19 million fortune is snatched from home, smuggled across the frontier and incarcerated. His captors try to force him to sign over the assets he controls. Interpol is alerted and a crack police unit frees him in a late night raid. It sounds like a B movie thrill, but the kidnap and rescue of 80-year-old Father Benjamin Videiro were only too real.

Once a powerhouse of religious activism in Asia, Macau's Jesuit community is still shocked by this bizarre twist in a dispute over control of one of its schools. The Melchior Carneiro Institute, which Father Videiro founded 37 years ago, is currently occupied by six rebel teachers who have locked out the Jesuits and launched a legal battle to gain control of it. The confrontation has provided a messy finale to Portuguese rule over the tiny enclave – and an inglorious addition to the Jesuits' record in the Orient.

Across the strait that separates Macau from the mainland, on Sancian Island, stands one of the most poignant memorials to Christianity in the Far East: a small white church, built to mark the place where St Francis Xavier died on his failed mission to bring Christianity to China almost half a millenium ago. The saint's bones have since been removed to Goa, but the church is a place of pilgrimage – despite the Chinese ban on a church that owes its allegiance to Rome, rather than Beijing.

Another monument to the struggle to christianise the Orient stands on the Macau peninsula: the baroque façade of the ruined church of St Paul, erected by Jesuits in 1565, a few decades after the colony was founded. Macau was to become the launch pad for four centuries of Jesuit activity. St Francis Xavier's successors – missionaries like Matteo Ricci – blazed evangelist trails across the celestial kingdom and, further afield, to Japan, Indochina, Laos and Cambodia. Only eight priests and one brother remain.

Father Videiro poured all his energy into establishing the Melchior Carneiro Institute as an institution that enshrined the Jesuit philosophy of education with a spiritual foundation. It occupies one of the best pieces of real estate in Macau – a site adjacent to the ruined church of St Paul – and Father Videiro's numerous trips abroad to solicit funds left the school with reserves of 56 million patacas (about US$7 million).

The value of the school site, around US$12 million with planning permission, and the wealth in its bank account led to the dispute that broke out three years ago when a group of staff sought to wrest financial control away from the priest. According to Father Manuel Texeira, a Portuguese priest, Father Videiro was submitted to increasing restrictions on his movements by the rebellious staff and became a virtual prisoner in the school compound. 'The whole affair was all about money,' he said. 'Father Videiro had been so successful in raising money for the school that he created expectations among a group of staff that they would one day be able to control that money, which had accumulated into a very large sum.'

Earlier last year Father Videiro's brother – also a priest, based in Portugal – became worried because he hadn't heard from him for some time. When he eventually managed to phone him in June, he heard a voice in the background saying: 'Tell him to go away'. He reported the matter to the Portuguese police. They asked Interpol to investigate and Father Videiro was eventually traced to a hotel in the Chinese city of Foshan – although there was no record of his ever having left Macau. Police later speculated that he had been smuggled out of Macau with the help of one of the enclave's Triads. Chinese police raided the hotel on 28 June and freed the Jesuit whose health had badly deteriorated. He was returned to Macau and admitted to hospital under police guard.

Macau police charged 10 teachers and other staff from the school in connection with the kidnapping. The staff, who have since been released on bail, claim they took Father Videiro to China for medical treatment. But Father Videiro said they tried to force him to sign a will giving them ownership of the school after his death. The priest's ordeal, however, was not yet over. While enjoying the sun in Macau's central Senado Square during an outing from hospital, three female members of the school staff made another attempt to snatch him by grabbing the handles of his wheelchair in a bid to push him towards a waiting car. Father Videiro has since returned to Portugal.

The Jesuits officially closed the school, but the six rebel teachers occupying the building are continuing to hold classes for about 300 students. The Jesuit Superior for Macau and Hong Kong, Father Alfred Deignan, said the order hoped to resolve the confrontation peacefully and would await the outcome of legal proceedings launched in connection with the control of the school. 'The efforts of the staff to get Father Videiro to sign the school over to them were pointless,' he said. 'The school is owned by the Jesuit order; it has never been the private possession of Father Videiro so he had no power it will it to anyone. Unfortunately we won't be able to resolve the matter and get the school reopened until the court case is settled. That could take years.' According to Father Texeira, Father Videiro had often acted as if the school was his own property and had, in the past, been at loggerheads with his superiors over his autocratic approach to its management.

The dispute comes at a time when the religious orders are seeing their influence wane in the once staunchly Catholic colony. The Jesuits still have three schools in Macau, but they may have to leave one, because the Carmelite nuns who own the land it stands on have packed up and gone to Canada. One priest, Father Luis Ruiz, is the founder of Caritas Macau and runs four homes for refugees, the handicapped and the elderly. Until recently he made regularly visits to leper colonies in southern China but these ended when the Chinese authorities revoked his visa. He is 86 years old and there are no younger priests coming from Europe to replace him.

'Our future in Macau will depend on whether we can maintain our manpower resources,' said Father Deignan. 'We're just not getting the vocations from European countries like we used to. Our traditional sources of young priests are drying up. At one stage, in Hong Kong we had about 100 Irish priests alone. Now there are about 30 Jesuits here in total. Our hope is that the Asian countries – South Korea, Indonesia, the Philippines – will make up the shortfall in vocations.' ❏

Barry Lowe *teaches journalism at the City University of Hong Kong*

MIA COUTO

A celebration in waiting

They may share a common language, but Portugal's erstwhile colonial subjects are still waiting for recognition of their rightful place in the history of the 'Discoveries'

The Discoveries have not been pacific. They have spoiled the whole issue. It needs cleaning, it needs polishing. Political and ideological abuses stained, deformed and afflicted that historical event. The glorification of the Discoveries served colonial elites who needed to give history a fresh coat; to sanction a 'mission', by endowing it with 'civilising' purposes. At the same time, it was also necessary to appease the blood, to hide the barbarism. Later on, during the post-colonial period, everybody had to accept that there had been something called 'unruliness'. An operation to recover history hastily presented as 'excesses' that which, after all, was intrinsic to a specific system.

But the mystification of the Discoveries – especially the processes initiated by them – was also convenient to the new African elites which needed an aura of victimisation. Instead of challenging the colonial ideology, their approach would go on to reinforce it. The formula of the absolute victim reduces Africans to the status of non-persons, amorphous objects incapable of generating their own conflicts. Blaming external factors – as if they were the only mechanism for these processes – helped nullify the domestic significance of their own internal contradictions. The demonisation of the stigma of 'evils' – always originating from outside – in the end sanctioned an inherently racist argument that robbed the Africans of their capacity to generate and manage their own conflicts. The presentation of Africans as an indistinct mass was a unified response to regain their lost dignity, but it ended up extinguishing deep cultural diversity. There is not one, but several, Africas. This continent cannot do without the right to plurality.

For all these reasons, the Discoveries are hardly a pacific theme. It will take time for us all to celebrate the historical events with equal liberty. Only when we all meet – these here and those there – people who shared the initiative and traded destinies. Let us discover each other. Lands are 'discovered', never cultures. Cultural legacies are handed over through long love affairs: they are not 'discovered', they are created. We are building up a category of relationship, acting upon the wounds and cicatrices of a very recent past. The solution of these traumas demands truth, demands the dialogue that yesterday was denied. What is the Europe that Africans know? What image of Africa today reaches Europeans? To whom do we hand this portrait of ourselves? To TV companies? To media groups whose art is to profit from that which they only simplify, reduce and disfigure?

I realise that the term 'Discoveries' has been downgraded in favour of another one: the 'convergence of cultures'. I have serious doubts about the reality of that convergence. Political regimes made that kind of convergence unfeasible. The trade was historically unattainable. Racial and cultural crossbreeding occurred punctually, but in spite of the colonial systems. It is not worth the trouble to compare those colonial systems to discover which was the more permissive. In all cases, cultural convergence was episodic, personal and dispersed.

As I said before, there was a lot of discovery in the so-called Discoveries. But which Africa was discovered or – converged upon? Who, for example, knows the religion (I should be using the plural) of African peoples? Don't these religions have a name? By default, and for the sake of convenience, they were called 'animist'. The rest was slung into the sack of 'cults', 'tribes, 'ethnic conflicts'. The knowledge of African cultures and philosophies is still an anthropological topic. Africa is the subject of ethnography, ethnology. It is the domain of 'Africanists'. It never happens the other way round. Africans do not study European tribes as an anthropological subject. They do not take the religions established in Europe as a topic. European art is not studied as folklore, or artisanal craft. There is not a hint in this unburdening of any bitterness or recrimination. Sadly, Africa has become exotic even to Africans.

Everything remains for us to do. We have to undertake deep cultural exchanges. This can not be achieved by sending art delegations on reciprocal visits. That is something, but it's not enough. We have to exchange systems of knowledge, strategies and sensibilities if we are to recreate the world. We have to learn to look into the history of our species with a different kind of eagerness. And to recognise that if – once brought to light – the Discoveries ought to be celebrated, other human epics, other achievements must be recovered from history.

One of these epics was the Diaspora which the pioneers of our species initiated from the African savannahs. That voyage – those Discoveries – put our ancestors in touch with new environments and initiated the settlement of regions never visited before by human beings. Distances on Earth were more extensive then than those which separate us from the moon. It was the first big step in man's humanisation and globalisation. This process of discovery formed traits in our character which we still preserve today. I dare say that those discoveries left a deeper and more lasting legacy than any other subsequent trip carried out by man. I hold no illusions that we will one day sing the glories of that remote epic. We are too tightly bound up in our modern image, too vain about technological supremacy to acknowledge how much we owe to something so familiar, but so difficult to endorse.

Celebrate the Discoveries? Yes, always. But more as a reciprocal process: a voyage in which all of us are the harbour and the destination, and as a conquest in which we all hold a stake. To celebrate the Portuguese navigators' voyages as a heroic feat, and whose culpability all of us have helped to remove. The discoveries of maritime routes were decisive events, conquests that belong to humanity. This commemoration will only be complete when ancient 'discoverers' and 'discovered' identify one another as the subjects of a new relationship. We do have to celebrate the journey still to be undertaken inside mankind. That voyage is still, and always, to be embarked upon. We have discovered terrestrial and maritime routes. Now we have to discover the human route to the future. ❏

Mia Couto has written six books of poetry, fiction and chronicles. Voices Made Night *(1990) and* Every Man is a Race *(1994) are published in translation by Heinemann. This essay, translated by Alejandra Guibert, was first printed in* Jornal de Letras, Artes e Ideias *in January 1997*

DAVID TOMORY

Reluctant heritage

'In 1498,' went the school mnemonic, 'Vasco da Gama knocked on India's gate.' In Goa you can still hear the knocking

It was obvious that the quincentenary of Vasco da Gama's arrival in India would be a fraught occasion when it was announced that a cultural troupe's visit to Portugal for the celebrations had been cancelled because of the withdrawal of government funding. Statements from Portugal stressed that the event would celebrate not the beginnings of imperialism, but the 'encounter of cultures'. The local press responded that this revisionism was no doubt a 'good thing', but that India would still not celebrate the arrival of her first European invader.

The anniversary flushed out a wide range of opinions. Historians were sage and empirical. Columnists and politicians were tough on colonialism. Anti-package-tour people called package tourism to Goa 'neo-colonialism'. Someone on an anti-Vasco protest described the condition of Goans under Portuguese rule as 'slavery'. Other Goans, resident and émigré, defended the colonial inheritance, while the Portuguese ambassador to India, interviewed in *Goa Today*, thought the resort's meandering back roads very 'old-style Portuguese' – and was diplomatic about the rest. Prone before the sea in the sun-stunned interval of their beach holidays, tourists pleaded ignorance of who Vasco da Gama was – except for one, who knew he played for a Brazilian football club.

One trouble was that the celebration squeezed the whole debate about Portugal's 451 years in Goa into an argument about a single person. Vasco made a big entrance. His irruption into the Indian Ocean as a late-fifteenth century son of the sword fixed Vasco in Indian history as a big, bad name – though his Empire of India was so insignificant that contemporary sources barely mention it. Compare the British arrival two centuries later: a modest affair of merchant adventurers on a muddy riverbank in Bengal that ended with the entire subcontinent being subjugated. But who remembers Job Charnock – or reviles him?

A Goan delegation travelled south to Calicut, where Vasco had actually arrived, to protest against the celebration. Vasco, a spokesman said, hadn't achieved even a nautical triumph. He didn't know the way; didn't have a map; he'd had to hire a pilot. A Portuguese tourist of Goan descent, also on his way to Calicut, said that of course Vasco didn't know the way: he was the first European to sail the Indian Ocean – for which there was no map in 1498, unless you meant the Ptolemaic one, or one of the old *mappae mundi* with Jerusalem at the top, Hell at the bottom and 'Here Be Dragons' in the middle. Obviously, he hired a pilot.

My interlocutor hadn't come to India with the quincentenary in mind, but the thought of being in Calicut pleased him. He considered it an historical occasion, and was puzzled by the protester's vehemence. 'You can't politicise things in 1998 that happened 500 years ago,' he insisted. 'Vasco wasn't a "colonialist": there was no concept of colonialism then, no nation-state to invade.'

He sailed for the glory of his faith – and because he was minor nobility, forever hanging round the palace in case the King needed something done. 'Some nautical experience' was all he had. You didn't set off for *Terra Incognita* in a leaky caravel unless you really needed work. Unwittingly he began European imperialism in Asia. Unintentionally he introduced Portugal to India. But the fact remains that he began 'our mutual heritage'.

The beauty of heritage – or the privately run heritage business – is that it doesn't depend on the past, offering only history without tragedy – the simple recreation of history's fun bits, such as food, costume, music and 'ambience'. Heritage is the old romantic stuff that nobody minds. You can't see it being as contentious in Goa as 'history' can be, but you never know: there have been protests against the lumpish copy of Vasco's flagship that stands on the beach at Cavelossim. 'But it isn't neo-colonialism,' its exasperated creator is reported to have said. 'It's concrete.'

Or it isn't history, it's heritage. Something concrete and beyond dispute. ❑

David Tomory *is the author of* A Season in Heaven *(Lonely Planet 1996)*

SOUSA JAMBA

A morsel of honey

The pleasures of a common language are not undiluted

Whenever I think of the Portuguese language, two scenes come to mind. The first is in 1973. I was aged seven and attending Escola de Fatima in Huambo on the Central Angolan plateau. One of the girls had spoken Umbundu – our native language – and a colleague had denounced her to the headmistress, a Catholic nun. The nun came over with a *palmatoria* (wooden ferule) and caned the girl in front of the school saying this was what would happen to anyone who dared to speak the 'forbidden language'. The second scene is in 1997 in a Lisbon apartment. My mother and her elderly friends were watching a video of Tchalo Dachala, a young Angolan poet. Tchalo was declaiming in Umbundu a long narrative poem that moved my mother and her friends to tears.

Tchalo was born in 1975, the year after Angola became independent. He had never suffered the humiliations others had gone through in the colonial era as they tried to acquire proficiency in Portuguese. Also, he is carrying on a trait that was common among Angolans – polyglotism. Tachalo speaks several other Angolan languages and he writes poems in Portuguese and English (a language he taught himself).

Many urban Angolans have chosen not to learn Bantu languages because it was, after all, not only people like my headmistress who insisted on us not speaking Umbundu; many parents who aspired to *assimilado* status dissuaded their children from speaking native languages. This linguistic snobbery has lingered on in post-colonial Angola. Citizens of middling education rarely talk to one another in African languages. And many Angolans who have mastered Portuguese, affect to sound as Portuguese as possible to prove their *assimilado* credentials. Angolans even have a special term for this expunging of Bantu influence in one's diction – *afinar a lingua* (sharpening the tongue).

Some years ago, at a dinner in Lisbon, a Portuguese journalist started mimicking an Angolan intellectual trying to sound white. I found the scene – which had other Portuguese in stitches – disconcerting because it reminded me of the Catch-22 situation many black Angolans lived through in the colonial days: the authorities encouraged them to be as Portuguese as possible; but when they did so there were laughed at by the Portuguese as *calçinhas* or 'uppity niggers'.

The white Angolan writer Costa da Andrade once noted that some of the most vocal critics of Portuguese culture were black Angolans who could not speak African languages and had lost links with the Bantu culture of the country. Angolans have not yet had the opportunity of exorcising the many demons left by the colonial experience. In the urban areas, there are still many people who view those in the interior as a benighted lot who will only 'come to the modern world' once they have mastered Portuguese, which remains the language of administrative and cultural power.

The debates in Angola about the role of indigenous languages must seem absurd to many Zambians, Malawians, Zimbabweans and even South Africans. In these countries, Bantu heritage remains a matter of fact. Young people learn English and other Bantu languages routinely. I grew up in Zambia as an Angolan refugee. Apart from English – the language with which I am most comfortable – I am fluent in three other Zambian languages. This is not unusual in that part of Africa. Yet many Angolans who are fluent in Russian, Bulgarian, Romanian, Serbo-Croat would need an interpreter to speak to their relatives in the interior.

If Angola is to come to terms with its many-layered identity, then it will have to admit its Bantu heritage and give the many Bantu languages their importance. In the dialogue between the urban and rural areas, it will not just be a matter of rural people acquiring the Portuguese language. Urban Angolans will also have to make the effort to learn African languages and delve into the imaginative worlds of these languages.

One exercise I often do is to compare the words of the different languages I know and think about the concepts behind them. One evening, I was cooking meat in my London flat when I tasted a morsel to find out whether it was ready. A voice in my head spoke against this and the Umbundu words *okuyanja* came to mind. This word has no equivalent in English or Portuguese. Roughly, it is a disapproving term

Remains of a Portuguese air force plane in Mozambique – Credit: Carlos Guarita

for the cook who keeps tasting the meal in the absence of others. But it also suggests the need to overcome your instincts. Suddenly, I felt privileged for having learned Umbundu and some of its intricacies.

An argument often cited in justifying the pre-eminence of Portuguese is that it is the sole factor that can unite Angolans in building a nation. In the absence of Portuguese, many paint a picture of complete chaos. This is untrue. In rural Angola, where I lived for over a year as an adult after I left Zambia, people speak different languages but they are able to understand one another because there is a tradition of polyglotism. In many regions, it is not unusual for an individual to be able to speak several languages, and this tradition has been going on for centuries.

The ardent defenders of the supremacy of Portuguese often say that it also enables those who have mastered it to partake in a cultural discussion with the rest of the world. True, some Angolan novelists, painters and musicians often get invited to conferences in Portugal and Brazil to talk about urban Angola. This, of course, is not a futile endeavour: urban Angola has produced a culture that has much going for it. Yet, the much-referred-to cultural dialogue in the Lusophone world is often one-way: Angolans will watch Brazilian soap operas, import Portuguese food and dance to Cape Verdian music without sending in turn anything substantial to these countries.

When Angolans refer to their literature, for instance, they usually have in mind the period spanning the late 19th century to the anti-colonial writings of the 1960s. Yet little is made of the vibrant oral tradition that remains intact in most of rural Angola. It is not unusual to hear Angolan writers say gleefully that they see themselves as carrying on with the tradition of Camões and Pessoa. However, other traditions are often discarded, and this disregard of anything African is sustained by many Angolans without blood-ties to Portugal.

In 1984, I was travelling deep in the Angolan bush with a couple of young men who had been raised in that milieu. These were men who knew the Umbundu name for each plant, bird, weed and root. I had just come from Zambia where I had done my O level exams, spoke English and Portuguese and thought of myself as immensely superior. After all, they had difficulties expressing themselves even in Portuguese. One afternoon, we got lost and we were hungry. I felt very weak and desperate. Suddenly, my colleagues found a tree and they knew at once that it contained wild honey. They started hacking away at the trunk and the honey came pouring out.

From then on I saw those young men in a different light. True, I had mastered books; but they had mastered the forest. I could read a compass, make sense of contours on a map. Yet they too had skills which helped us along. If the urban could turn to the rural areas with similar openness, Angola might be able to overcome its present identity crisis. ❏

Sousa Jamba is a London-based novelist and journalist. He has written two novels, Patriots *(Viking) and* A Lonely Devil *(Fourth Estate). He has just completed a novel about Africans in London*

JOSE RAMOS-HORTA

The road to Alas

Michael Griffin: *What were you doing when news of the Carnation Revolution was announced in Dili in 1974?*

José Ramos-Horta: I had packed, sold the few things I had to raise some money and was going to leave for Australia. A few months earlier, I'd given an interview to an Australian newspaper in which I'd talked about independence for East Timor. This greatly displeased the government. On 25 April, news of the coup came and I was allowed to stay. It would have been my second exile. In 1970, I'd spent the evening in Dili with a tourist from New Jersey. We were drinking and I made a speech criticising Portugal's 'civilising mission'. I want to put this on record because I don't want to be a false hero. If I had not been utterly drunk, I would never have had the guts to say what I did. So my exile was largely the result of one drinking binge.

Could you compare the diplomacy of Portugal and Brazil in bringing East Timor's case to the UN's attention?

Brazil played no significant role. The countries that most supported us were the African Portuguese-speaking countries. From 1975 till the late 1980s, when Portugal really jumped in, it was Angola, Cape Verde, Mozambique, Guinea-Bissau and São Tomé that saved us. Brazil always voted for self-determination but it never played a more significant role although, in the last few years, there has been a mushrooming of solidarity groups.

East Timorese resistance to the Portuguese was as fierce in its day as resistance has been to Indonesian rule over the past 25 years. Is there something in the culture that identifies with Portuguese mores, language and religion - the West, rather than the East - or is the battle solely for independence?

Resistance to Portuguese rule was primarily in the nineteenth century but the relationship changed. It was not a typical colonial relationship. There were no Portuguese planters, very few civil servants and the island, after World War II, was extremely peaceful. Because Portugal was far away, a cordial relationship was forged between its remotest colony and the Metropole. The language is spoken only by the minority, but the influence is strong in other ways: the spread of the Catholic faith, for instance, and possibly the East Timorese temperament. They like soccer, unlike most South East Asian countries; they enjoy Portuguese music and dance; and above all, there is a deep sense of dignity. The East Timorese can be patient but, when it is a matter of honour, they get extraordinarily resistant.

Could an independent East Timor make a viable economic unit? Is some form of autonomy within a federal Indonesia the most likely way forward?

What are the advantages of joining a bankrupt country? Indonesia cannot even feed its own people, so why should we join them? When people talk of pragmatism, I ask: 'What are the incentives for joining Indonesia?' We'd be better off joining Australia: that would be a persuasive argument from a pragmatic point of view. Join Indonesia? We might as well join Bangladesh! Apart from that, East Timor can survive as well as Fiji, Luxembourg and other small countries. We have oil, natural gas and very determined people.

What were you doing on 21 May 1998 when President Suharto of Indonesia stepped down from power?

It was three in the morning. I was fast asleep when a phone call came telling me to listen to Suharto's resignation speech. I was elated. Two years earlier, in May 1996, I'd given an interview to CNN in which I predicted that Suharto would fall in two years. I was right on target.

You frequently say that the joint 1996 Nobel Peace Prize to you and Bishop Carlos Belo rightfully belongs to Xanana Gusmão, the resistance leader imprisoned since 1992 and often described as the 'Mandela of East Timor'. What is his current physical condition and what role could he play in a resolution to the current stand-off over East Timor?

He is in very good health and strong in spirit. Though still in prison in Jakarta, he is very active, receiving a stream of visitors from East Timor, Indonesia and overseas. Mandela has been to see him. This all testifies to his international standing. Everybody agrees that he holds the key to a peaceful resolution to the conflict. Indonesia should allow him to go home to his people, because they trust him. He is a moderate and a pragmatist, capable of calming down the increasingly restless and angry East Timorese.

Do you believe that the UN, USA, Portugal, Indonesia and Australia are now converging on agreement? Is self-determination more likely now than five years ago?

Absolutely. Independence is now only a matter of time. The decisions of the USA and Australia are now closer to what I have advocated for many years: a step-by-step approach, starting with the release of prisoners and demilitarisation, a genuine local autonomy with international guarantees and, finally, a referendum to determine the final status of the territory. This is the only formula by which Indonesia can disengage with honour and dignity.

UN investigators tried to gain access to sites of recent alleged massacres of civilians, notably in Alas. Is Indonesia more willing to accept outside scrutiny in East Timor?

They did not allow the former UN Secretary General to go to Alas, which makes us worried that there has been a far greater massacre than has been reported. What were they afraid of? What were they hiding? Bishop Belo told me an official delegation from Dili, comprising the puppet governor, the local church and some NGOs, attempted to go to Alas. They were fired on by the military and forced to return. Bishop Belo's information is that at least 40 people were slaughtered in Alas. ❏

José Ramos-Horta has spent the past 24 years denouncing Indonesia's illegal invasion of East Timor on 7 December 1975. This triggered the slaughter of an estimated 200,000 people by 1979. With Bishop Carlos Filipe Ximenes Belo, he shared the 1996 Nobel Peace Prize. Interview by **Michael Griffin**

Composed around the echo of a pistol shot

History has a fearful symmetry. Our century opened with a pistol shot in Sarajevo and ends, once more, to the sound of gunfire in the Balkans. The 'sick man of Europe' – the ailing Turkish empire that reached from Istanbul to the gates of Vienna – is long dead; the spoils of it dispersed. Another World War and the end of another empire of sorts have released all the old demons and brought the powers rushing to the spot to ensure that the Balkan imbroglio does not once again endanger the security of Europe.

It's all about 'peace' in our world, in our time. First it was Bosnia; now it's Kosovo. It could yet be Montenegro or Vojvodina. And – *pace* the fireworks in Iraq – while the world was watching Kosovo in the hope of a deal that would end the slaughter, Milosevic applied his peace-making skills closer to home.

The 'pacification' of the university, a seat of past troubles that had the temerity not only to criticise but to challenge the regime in power, was high on the agenda. In October, a new law governing the universities, enabled the government to reassert control and saw dissenting professors teaching on the street and students reviving the defunct resistance that had brought crowds of 100,000 and more onto the streets in 1996-97. In November, the application of a new Law on Public Information saw newspapers seized, closed, their editors dragged into court and fined impossible sums – often in absentia for the want of warning which they may have heard only accidentally and in retrospect – and 'repossessed' by state media operations from which they had liberated themselves in the early-1990s. Others are being driven to operate across the frontier in Montenegro – independent from Serbia in all but name – or face bankruptcy through financial harassment. *(Index Index p98)*.

Like the press, the long-suffering but resourceful and resilient independent radio and TV network operating under the umbrella of Association of Independent Electronic Media (ANEM), has been the butt of Milosevic's malice ever since its first, fragile attempts to counter the hate journalism of the official media that was largely responsible for the fear and hysteria that led to war with Croatia and Bosnia. For the past five years he has used every device to put

ANEM out of business: licences have been refused, frequencies denied; stations have been closed, their equipment seized and destroyed. The retransmission of news from the 'agents of foreign imperialism' – the BBC, Voice of America, Radio Free Europe, Deutsche Welle – was forbidden in November. Only its superior understanding of the possibilities of new communications technology keeps the network one step – just – ahead of the authorities.

Substitute Albanians for Bosnians and the language of the hate media is unchanged. The difference is that the tiny voice of ANEM now covers around 60 per cent of Serbia and has an audience of 1.6 million. This is what Milosevic fears and will do everything in his power to silence. ❏

JVH

PUNCH, OR THE LONDON CHARIVARI.—December 18, 1912.

SUBJECT TO CORRECTION.

Europa. "NOW THEN, GET ON WITH YOUR MAPS, AND WHEN YOU'VE FINISHED THEM BRING THEM TO ME AND I'LL SHOW YOU WHERE YOU'VE GONE WRONG!"

A censorship chronicle incorporating information from the American Association for the Advancement of Science Human Rights Action Network (AAASHRAN), Amnesty International (AI), Article 19 (A19), the BBC Monitoring Service Summary of World Broadcasts (SWB), the Committee to Protect Journalists (CPJ), the Canadian Committee to Protect Journalists (CCPJ), the Inter-American Press Association (IAPA), the International Federation of Journalists (IFJ/FIP), the International Federation of Newspaper Publishers (FIEJ), Human Rights Watch (HRW), the Media Institute of Southern Africa (MISA), International PEN (PEN), Open Media Research Institute (OMRI), Reporters Sans Frontières (RSF), the World Association of Community Broadcasters (AMARC), the World Organisation Against Torture (OMCT) and other sources

ALGERIA

On 14 October four national dailies, *El-Watan*, *Le Matin*, *Le Soir d'Algérie* and *La Tribune*, were instructed by the state printing presses to pay all outstanding debts within 48 hours in violation of an earlier agreement that involved staggered payment of debts. The printers' U-turn appears to be linked to four papers' critical coverage of recent ruling party infighting. As a mark of protest, three other leading dailies, *Liberté*, *El-Khabar* and *Le Quotidien d'Oran*, joined the strike, leaving the news stands empty of seven national dailies on 17 October. The striking newspapers resumed publication on 8 November. (RSF, HRW)

ARGENTINA

On 29 September the Supreme Court ordered actress **Gabriela Acher**, scriptwriter **Maitena Burundarena** and Channel 13 television network to pay damages of US$30,000 to a judge in connection with a sketch about justice aired in 1991 on the programme *Hagamos El Humor* (Let's Make Humour). (Periodistas)

On 20 October the Supreme Court overruled a one-month sentence awarded against journalist **Tomas Sanz**, former editor of the magazine *Humor*, for his article 'Two years of corruption', deemed offensive by then Senator Eduardo Menem. (Periodistas)

On 22 November an anonymous caller warned the daily *Clarín* that a bomb had been placed in the building. After a three-hour search, journalists returned to work though the scare delayed the next day's edition. (Periodistas)

On 23 November the daily *Pagina/12* obtained evidence of espionage by Air Force Intelligence against the newspapers *Clarín*, *La Nación*, *Cronista* and *Pagina/12*. One of the documents found contained information about journalists **Ronaldo Barbano**, **Alcadio Oña**, **Roberto Solans**, **Carlos Rodríguez**, **José E. Toyah**, **Hernán Firpo**, **Adrian Ventura**, **Alfredo Vega**, **Sergio Moreno** and **Dolores Oliveira**. They had all criticised airport security and a forthcoming privatisation. In September 1997 an Austral Airlines airplane crash in Uruguay killed everyone on board. (Periodistas)

ARMENIA

The Yerevan Press Club issued a statement on 19 October decrying parliamentary interference in the media. 'First the National Assembly has mandated the day and time that "Parliamentary Hour" should be broadcast on television, interfering in the programme policy of Armenian National Television ... Then the speaker of the Armenian National Council dismisses the editor-in-chief of *Ayastani Anrapetutyun* newspaper, Liza Chagaryan, giving justifications which smack of censorship.' (SWB)

AZERBAIJAN

Press freedom groups and the US State Department condemned the beating of journalists by police during unsanctioned demonstrations in Baku on 7 and 8 November. The interior ministry responded with a letter denying that police used violence during the demonstrations and condemning the State Department's assertions as a 'fabrication.' (RFE/RL)

Ilham Saban, a journalist for the Turan news agency, was beaten by police as he covered an opposition rally in Baku on 9 November, despite having shown his press card to a police officer. (RSF)

Three months after 'abolishing press censorship', parliament issued a statement on 10 November calling on the information ministry to take 'all legal measures' to preclude the publication of 'unconfirmed and provocative materials' and to 'defend the honour and dignity of the president'. On 13 November deputies passed legislation limiting the right to hold public demonstrations. On 24 November they voted by 80 to seven to impose prison sentences of up to three years for organising, or participating in, an unsanctioned demonstration. (Reuters, Turan, ITAR-TASS, Interfax)

On 12 November, *Yeni Musavat* Editor **Rauf Arifoglu** and three colleagues stopped eating in protest at government harassment. The provocation was a libel case against *Yeni Musavat*, in which two presidential aides allege the paper published uncorroborated allegations against them by opposition presidential candidates. One week later, 21 other editors of independent newspapers joined the protest fast, now also in support of *Azadliq* newspaper, which stands accused of 'insulting the honour and dignity of President Heidar Aliyev'. Journalists from *Yeni Musavat* and *Azadliq* have been beaten, harassed and arrested repeatedly in recent months (*Index* 4/1998). Meeting with Arifoglu and *Azadliq* editor **Gunduz Tairli** on 18 November, Prosecutor-General Eldar Hasanov offered to drop the criminal cases and to impose only minimal fines if the editors published apologies. The offer was rejected. Hasanov reminded the editors that President Aliyev personally controlled the media and the right of Azerbaijani citizens to free speech. By 21 November, those pledged to the hunger strike included several opposition politicians and 'thousands of readers'. On 1 December, the editors ended their hunger strike, to be replaced by their deputies and the entire editorial staff of the newspaper *Cumhuriyet*. (Turan, Reuters, ANS-Press, Interfax, RFE/RL)

Former president **Abulfaz Elchibey**, chairman of the Azerbaijan Popular Front Party (APFP), was charged on 13 November with defaming the honour and dignity of his successor as president, Heidar Aliyev, a crime punishable by up to six years in prison. Elchibey had affirmed in articles published in the opposition newspapers *Azadliq* and *Yeni Musavat* that Aliyev was instrumental in the creation of Turkey's Kurdistan Workers' Party (PKK). Elchibey later declined to institute libel proceedings against the government newspaper *Yeni Azerbaycan* in relation to a 17 November story that claimed his party was working actively with the PKK. The article alleged that an APFP emissary had departed for Rome to plot the sabotage of the planned Baku-Ceyhan oil export pipeline with detained PKK chairman Abdullah Öcalan. (Turan, Reuters, Interfax)

Four female journalists from *Yeni Musavat* were beaten in front of the Supreme Court in Baku on 16 November. **Smira Mamigdze, Ilhame Mamigdze, Zamina Alligudze** and '**Ainur**' were injured as police violently dispersed a group of journalists who were protesting against a defamation lawsuit brought against Rauf Arifoglu, the newspaper's editor. (OMCT, RSF)

On 19 November a Baku court imposed a 20 million manat (US$5,000) fine on *Yeni Musavat* for having implicated a senior Azerbaijani Interior Ministry official in the February 1997 murder of academic **Zia Buniatov**. Vidadi Mahmudov, *Yeni Musavat*'s defence lawyer, complained that the verdict was unfair since the newspaper had also carried a statement by the official denying any part in the killing. (Turan, RFE/RL)

On 25 November, police broke up a picket in front of the presidential administration building in Baku in support of the ongoing editors' hunger strike. **Asif Marzili** of *Tadlar* newspaper, **Nizami Mokhammedali** of *Radikal* and **Anar Alipoladoglu** of *Mustagil* were beaten and injured by police, who also detained four employees of *Yeni Musavat* and confiscated camera equipment from a *Megapolis* reporter. (RSF, RFE/RL)

Thirteen separate libel cases have been lodged against the newspaper *Azadliq* for a total of US$462,000 in damages, it was reported on 25 November. The cases have been brought by senior officials and members of President Aliyev's family, including his brother Djalal, whom *Azadliq* claimed has bought expensive property in the UK. (RFE/RL, Turan)

OSCE Chairman Bronislaw Geremek explained to President Aliyev during a 26 November visit to Baku that suing opposition newspapers for libel was strongly at odds with the government's avowed commitment to free speech. Aliyev rejected the arguments of Geremek, who later visited the editors on hunger strike. Geremek suggested they should end their fast, having 'demonstrated the dramatic state of freedom of speech in Azerbaijan'. (*Neue Zürcher Zeitung*, RFE/RL)

Fuad Gakhramanly, a senior APFP member, was sentenced to 18 months in prison on 27 November after being convicted of sedition. The conviction relates to an unpublished article, 'Meeting Tactics of the Opposition', confiscated when police raided the independent newspaper *Chag* in June 1998. The prosecution claims the document was intended as a blueprint for overthrowing the government and was drafted by a think-tank affiliated with the APFP. Senior party members have denied the existence of such a think-tank. A US State Department spokesman condemned the conviction of Gakhramanly, and the government's broader campaign to 'harass the opposition and restrict freedom of thought and expression'. (Turan, Reuters, AP, RFE/RL)

BANGLADESH

Author **Taslima Nasrin** (*Index* 10/ 1993, 3/1994,

4/1994, 5/94, 6/1994, 1/1995, 2/1995, 6/1996, 2/1997, 6/1998) was granted bail on 22 November by the High Court in Dhaka in relation to the charges of blasphemy against her. The court also ruled that she would not have to appear in person during the pending trial because her life could be in danger. Nasrin returned from four years of exile this autumn to look after her dying mother. (BBC World Service)

BENIN

On 17 November **Maurice Chabi** and **Pascal Zantou**, chief editor and reporter, respectively, for the independent daily *Les Echos du Jour*, received a six-month prison sentence for slander. The sentence followed the filing of a complaint by national Education Minister Léonard Padonou Jijoho. The minister took exception to an article in the 26 August edition that accused him of misappropriation of public funds. It has been over a year since any journalist has received a prison sentence. (RSF)

BRAZIL

Photojournalist **Miguel Pereira de Melo** was gunned down on 5 November in the Amazon state of Para, dying a day later in hospital. The killing took place to prevent the journalist testifying at a trial involving 159 police officers accused of massacring landless farm workers during a protest in Eldorado de Carajas in 1996. Pereira's pictures of the victims' bodies piled in a

truck were published around the world. (Freedom Forum)

BRUNEI

On 18 November the UK Law Lords voted unanimously to prevent accountants KPMG from investigating further the personal financial affairs of Prince Jeffri, estranged brother of the Sultan of Brunei. The ruling opens the way for the Law Lords to give guidance on the effectiveness of 'Chinese Walls',used by accountants to ensure client confidentiality. *(Financial Times)*

BULGARIA

On 21 October chief prosecutor Nestor Nesterov announced the state was closing the file on the murder of dissident **Georgi Markov**, as the time limit for the investigation had expired. **Markov**, a freelancer who worked for the BBC, was killed with a poison—tipped umbrella in London 1978. British Foreign Secretary Robin Cook said in Sofia that 'Communism has gone away with its secrets and the Markov case is one of them'. (RFE/RL)

BURMA

It was reported on 30 November that pro-democracy leader **Aung San Suu Kyi** had accused the ruling military of attempting to silence the National League for Democracy (NLD) movement by refusing to grant visas to visiting journalists unless they promised not to contact Suu Kyi (*Index* 2/1998, 5/1998). (Reuters)

CAMBODIA

On 4 October the pro-government daily *Rasmei Kampuchea* (Light of Cambodia) quoted Secretary of State for Information Khieu Khanarith as saying that the government planned to shut down the *Cambodian Daily* and *Phnom Penh Post* - two independent English-language newspapers that *Rasmei Kampuchea* has accused of biased and anti-government coverage. Khanarith was also reported as saying that British and US journalists would temporarily have to leave the country because they had incurred the wrath of 'the masses' and the government 'cannot protect them' (*Index* 5/1998). (CPJ)

The 1998 International Consortium of Investigative Journalists' (ICIJ) Award for Outstanding Investigative Reporting was presented to journalist **Nate Thayer** on 7 November for his exclusive reports on the late Khmer leader Pol Pot. They had 'illuminated a page of history that would have been lost to the world had he not spent years in the Cambodian jungle'. (ICIJ)

CAMEROON

Soter Agbaw Ebaï, a reporter with the thrice-weekly *Herald*, was arrested on 3 November and is being held under a committal order at the police station in Yaoundé. The arrest followed a libel compliant lodged against Ebaï by the former minister of higher education, Peter Agbor Tabi. Last August, the *Herald*

published an article which stated that Tabi had fled to Nigeria shortly after being relieved of his duties. (RSF)

On 12 November **Christopher Ezieh**, correspondent with the *Herald*, was detained at the police station in Kumba. The arrest followed the publication a day earlier of an article in which Ezieh alleged Governor Peter Acham had ordered a 60 per cent reduction in salary for Kumba's civil servants. (RSF)

Despite having his one-year sentence confirmed by the Supreme Court on 17 September this year, prisoner of conscience **Pius Njawe** (*Index* 3/1998 4/998 5/1998 6/1998) was granted a presidential pardon and released from imprisonment on 12 October. (AI, WAN)

CANADA

Newspaper publisher **Tara Singh Hayer** was gunned down outside his home in Surrey, British Columbia, on 18 November as he was returning from the offices of his newspaper, the *Indo-Canadian Times*, Canada's oldest Punjabi weekly. Hayer was an outspoken critic of fundamentalists who have periodically terrorised the Sikh community in the Vancouver area. Hayer, partially paralysed in a 1988 assassination attempt, was shot getting out of his car and into a wheelchair. His is the first case of a journalist murdered for his work in Canada this century. (CCPJ)

CHILE

The arrest of former General Augusto Pinochet on 16 October in London triggered a death threat against journalist **Hector Reinaldo Pavelic Sanhueza**, cousin of William Miller Sanhueza who disappeared in 1973. He was warned he would be killed if anything happened to Pinochet. On 23 October former political prisoner **Marta San Martin Alarcón** received a phone call warning her that 'her two sons were going to die'. In the same week, the daughter of painter and lecturer **José Balmes** received a call stating her father would be 'gutted' if the detention of former Pinochet continued. (Equipo Nizkor)

CHINA

Jurgen Kremb, correspondent for the German weekly *Der Spiegel*, was interrogated by officers from Beijing's State Security Bureau on 17 November. A day later, he was ordered to leave China within 48 hours on the grounds that he had 'possession of state secrets'. Kremb has written a book on his friend Wei Jingsheng which has recently become available in Chinese in Taipei. (RSF)

About 140 members of underground Protestant churches were arrested on 26 October and 5 November in the cities of Wugang and Nanyang in Henan province where they were holding meetings. **Cheng Meiying**, an activist who helped found underground churches for

China's estimated 11 million Protestants, was left with serious head injuries after being beaten with a water-soaked rope whip and a police baton. Meiying was subsequently released, but more then 70 church leaders were still in detention on 26 November. (Associated Press)

The first case involving the use of the internet for political purposes came before the court on 4 December. **Lin Hai** was arrested in March and accused of 'subverting the socialist system' by supplying numerous e-mail addresses to the overseas dissident publication *VIP Reference*, enabling it to bypass the censor. The trial will be closed to the public as it 'involves government internal affairs' according to a spokesman for the Shanghai foreign affairs office. (*Guardian*)

COLOMBIA

José Arturo Guapacha, director of the local bi-monthly magazine *Panorama*, was shot dead on 15 October. Guapacha, who was attacked by a gunman near a garage exit, had been practising journalism for 20 years and worked for the RCN and Todelar radio stations. (RSF)

Radio Caracol challenged a three-day closure order and kept working on 29 October. The sanctions were ordered by the Ministry of Communications after sports commentator **Edgar Perea** urged listeners to vote for the Liberal presidential candidate. (CPJ)

Two radio sports reporters for RCN in the Cali province were detained accused of accepting bribes of US$5,000 from a drug cartel. Journalists **Vicente Gallego** and **Esteban Jaramillo** were arrested on 16 and 18 October respectively and are being held without bail while awaiting trial. (Freedom Forum)

CROATIA

On 28 October a Zagreb district attorney asked the court to begin investigating **Slaven Letica** on possible charges of slandering President Franjo Tudjman. Letica, a professor of medicine, political columnist and former chief aide to the president, told the Slovenian weekly *Mladina* that 'Tudjman loves deviant types. He feels a certain attraction to ... criminals, paramilitary criminals, prostitutes. These people fascinate him, because they bring some fun into his boring, bureaucratic life'. (RFE/RL)

CUBA

The four leaders of the Internal Dissidents' Working Group for the Analysis of the Cuban Socio-Economic Situation (GTDI), **Felix A. Bonne Carcases**, **Vladimiro Roca Antunez**, **María Beatríz Roque Cabello**, **René Gomez Manzano**, were charged with sedition on 15 October. Prosecutors asked for a six-year sentence for Roca Antunez and five-year sentences for the others. The four were arrested on 16 July 1997, following a press conference in which they criticised an official document entitled 'The Party of Unity, Democracy and the Human Rights We Defend'. (AAASHRAN)

On 9 November the Government approved Associated Press' request to reopen its bureau, 29 years after the news agency was expelled from the island. CNN is the only US-based news organisation with a permanent presence, having opened a bureau in Havana in March last year. (Freedom Forum)

CZECH REPUBLIC

On 17 November the government was urged to ensure an immediate and thorough investigation into the attack on **Michal Klima**, managing director of the *Economia* newspaper. While the motive remained unclear, the attack was thought to have been related either to his publishing activities, or his position as chairman of Ceska Typografie, a printing plant where management corruption had been revealed. Two masked men attempted to put a rope around his neck on 9 November, but they were scared off before they could lead him to a waiting car. (WAN)

On 25 November Czech TV dismissed **Jan Stern**, producer of the popular investigative weekly programme *Nadoraz*, for committing 'a breach of the rules of objectivity, impartiality and balance of views'. Stern defended the accuracy of the programme and claimed he had been dismissed unlawfully, and that he had been under increasing pressure to eschew politically sensitive issues. Staff editors

Lubor Kohout and **Josef Viewegh**, and staff presenter **Rebeka Krizanova** soon followed Stern, while seven freelance reporters also resigned in protest. (Czech TV)

DEMOCRATIC REPUBLIC OF CONGO

The editor of the independent *Le Peuple* newspaper, **Paulin Tusumba Nkazi A Kanda**, was arrested at his home on 16 October for publishing a list of 29 people who had allegedly financed the rebellion against President Laurent Kabila's government. By 9 November Tusumba was reported to have appeared before the appeals court only once. (*CPJ*)

Clovis Mwamba Kayembe, a journalist with the opposition *L'Alarme* newspaper, was detained on 21 October for an article he wrote concerning the departure for Belgium of Interior Minister Gaetan Kakudji. (CPJ)

On 29 October rebels opposed to President Kabila's government are reported to have lifted a communication ban and allowed NGOs operating in north and south Kivu to use their own communications equipment. The use of international telephone lines was also allowed but only for 'humanitarian purposes'. (IRIN).

Jean-Marie Nkanku, a journalist with the weekly *L'Alerte*, was arrested on 30 October and taken to the military office for Anti-Patriotic Activities (DEMIAP) for publishing a photo of interior minister Gaetan Kakudji with rebel leader Zahidi Ngoma under the heading 'Gaetan Kakudji in the Arms of Zahidi Ngoma'. (*CPJ, RSF*)

The weekly *La Flamme du Congo* ceased publication on 3 November after its two journalists, **Gustave Kalenga** and **Kabago Mbaya**, were arrested by armed individuals in civilian clothes and detained at Kin Maziere police detention centre. In its 20 October edition the paper had published an article condemning alleged bribes involving president Kabila's cabinet chief. (RSF)

Kileba Poke Ame, editor-in-chief of the independent *Le Soft* newspaper, went into hiding on 5 November, while three of the newspaper's reporters, **Awazi Kharomon**, **Lubamba Lutoko** and **Bebe Ediya**, were detained for two days by members of the Rapid Intervention Police. Three other *Le Soft* employees, **Ricky Milunda**, **Buka**, **Freddy**, and a visitor, **Kenda Waling**, were also detained The newspapers had promised in its 3 November edition to publish an 'important document' on 6 November on the joint venture between Gécamines, the state-owned diamond marketing firm, the private company Ridgepoint and the minister who signed the agreement. Police raided and closed the newspaper before the 6 November edition and accused the journalists of reporting 'nonsense and excelling at misinformation'. (*CPJ, RSF*)

It was reported on 19 November that the editor of *La Libre Afrique*, **Loseke Lisumbou**, who was detained by security forces at the national security council (CNS) headquarters in late August had still not been released or charged in court. Lisumbou had been detained in connection with an article published in the newspaper reporting on the flight from the country tof he security adviser and chief of CNS. Despite a retraction by the newspaper, Lisumbou had neither been charged nor released. (*CPJ*).

Belmonde Magloire Missinhoun, a citizen of Bénin and owner of the financial newspaper *La Pointe Congo*, was reported missing on 19 November. He was allegedly arrested by police on 3 September after a traffic accident with a military vehicle but by 19 November he had not been traced and was feared dead. Missinhoun had lived in Kinshasa for 30 years and *La Pointe Congo* was alleged to have had close ties with the Mobutu regime. (*CPJ*)

On 19 November rebels fighting president Laurent Kabila are reported to have launched a news service. The rebel communication spokesman Prof Etienne Ngangura told Radio Bukavu that no journalists would be arrested while carrying out his/her duty 'even if their opinion was erroneous'. (IRIN)

Michel Musewe Diawe, a journalist with Congolese National Radio and

Television, was detained at Kokolo military camp on 21 November for having quit his position at the state television. His whereabouts remain unknown (CPJ)

EGYPT

Conservative theologian **Yeha Ismail** and *Al Ahrar* journalist **Mustafa Ibrahim** will be tried for libelling the Sheikh of Al Azhar, Mohammad Sayed Tantawi, state prosecutor Rigaa Al Arabi announced on 12 October. Ibrahim had quoted Ismail in an article criticising Tantawi for having permitted the movie *Devil's Advocate* to be shown in Egypt (*Index* 6/1998). (*Cairo Times*)

On 22 October **Mustafa Bakri**, editor-in-chief of *Al Osboa*, and his brother **Mahmoud** were convicted of libel by a Cairo criminal court and sentenced to a year in prison with hard labour. The court also ordered them to pay the legal expenses to the litigant, Mohammed Abel Aal, former head of the Social Justice Party. In a surprise move, however, chief public prosecutor Ragaa Al Arabi suspended the jail term on 24 October giving the Bakri brothers 60 days to appeal. (*Cairo Times*)

On 21 November the Helwan Court of Misdemeanours ruled that a case brought by the Centre for Human Rights and Legal aid challenging the constitutionality of the imprisonment of journalists would be heard by the High Constitutional Court. The decision has been hailed as a victory for freedom of the press (*Cairo Times*)

A new newspaper, *Al Geel* (Regeneration), largely modelled on the banned popular weekly *Al Dastour*, has hit the news stands. *Al Dastour* was banned in February (*Index* 3/1998) and efforts to revive the banned weekly under the *Alf Laila* title came to nothing. (*Cairo Times*)

On 1 December, the public prosecutor ordered the imprisonment of **Hafez Abu Saed**, secretary general of the Egyptian Organisation for Human Rights (EOHR) on charges of 'accepting funds from a foreign country with the aim of carrying out acts harmful to Egypt' and 'disseminating information inimical to national interests'. His arrest arose out of EOHR's recent report on torture. As publication of the report coincided with the disbursement of the grant from UK government, the authorities were quick to establish a connection. However, on the afternoon of 6 December, The Higher State Security Prosecution ordered Abu Saeda's release on bail. (A19, Egyptian Organisation for the Human Rights)

ERITREA

Ruth Simon, an Agence France Presse correspondent imprisoned since April 1997, is one of the five winners of the 1998 CPJ International Press Freedom Award (*Index* 4/1998, 5/1998). (CPJ)

Recent publications: *Eritrea: Even the Stones Are Burning* by Roy Rateman, (Red Sea Publications (revised edition), 239 pp)

ETHIOPIA

Tamrat Serbesa, the editor-in-chief of *Wonchif* weekly, is still being held at the Central Criminal Investigation office prison at Maekewi. He was arrested on 16 October and charged with libel for claiming in a report that President Negasso Gidada had been drunk at a gathering of Oromos. (*CPJ*)

An ndependent Amharic newspaper, *Nishan*, has reportedly ceased publication after the detention of its three journalists: **Shimelis Kemal**, editor-in-chief, his deputy **Berhanu Negash** and **Teferi Mekonnen**, editor. The three were detained on 13 July and released on 19 October after being questioned about an editorial they had published cautioning against hate propaganda against Eritreans. As a result, the publication's sole financial backer withdrew his support and the publishers lost the lease on their editorial offices. (*CPJ*)

On 29 October it was reported that **Samson Seyum**, editor-in-chief of the Amharic weekly *Goh*, was still being held at an unknown location together with **Tilahun Bekele**, editor-in-chief of the Amharic weekly *Fetash*. The two are alleged to have defamed the newly established Crown Mineral Water Factory. (*RSF*)

EUROPEAN UNION

The row over EU financial corruption continued in

October when Commission President Jaques Santer was forced to open EU accounts to parliamentary scrutiny. The move followed allegations of fraud relating to the ECHO food aid programme, dating back to 1994 and involving Ecu 2.4 billion. MEPs had threatened to block any discussions on future EU development aid budget committments if the accounts were not laid open to scrutiny. This dispute continues a bad year for the EU which is currently investigating 950 cases of fraud. (*EP News*)

On 9 October the EU was criticised by *Guardian* journalist **Martin Walker** for toning down a disparaging report on human rights implementation by member states. The initial report had called for the establishment of a specific human rights coordinating department with its own commissioner. The first draft also made reference to 'inhumane and degrading treatment of detainees' with regard to asylum seekers. The final report features heavily reduced proposals calling for a human rights commissioner, but no special department. The report does say, however, that EU human rights policies are 'ambivalent, incoherent and effectively in disarray'. (*Guardian*)

It was reported on 26 October that two EU member countries are challenging the EU in the European Court of Justice. Germany has brought a case disputing the ban on tobacco advertising. The case has two main threads: first, that promotion of public health is the responsibility of

national governments and, secondly, that the ban on advertising contravenes the right to free speech. The second case has been brought by the Dutch government, which is challenging the EU directive that allows the patenting of discoveries of plant and animal forms. The Dutch argue that the EU has exceeded its powers by passing a law that conflicts with human rights law and international treaties. (*European*)

FRANCE

On 19 November a French court ruled that former MI5 officer **David Shayler** could not be extradited to London for breach of the Official Secrets Act (*Index 5/1998*). John Wadham, director of the civil rights group Liberty and Shayler's lawyer, described the court's decision as a 'marvellous victory for freedom of speech'. (*Guardian*)

GEORGIA

Aleko Tskitishvili, a reporter for *Resonance* newspaper, was beaten and kicked by special police forces commanded by Temur Mgebrishvili as he tried to enter the Supreme Court building for the last day of the trial of Mkhedroni paramilitary leaders on 10 November, coincidentally Georgia's 'Police Day'. Tskitishvili was detained for three hours at Mtatsminda police station where Mgebrishvili again beat him. The Mtatsminda procurator's office announced it would be investigating the incident, but when journalists from

Rustavi-2 TV channel tried to cover Mgebrishvili's questioning on 16 November, they were ejected from the procurator's office by special police. (*Sakartveli Gazeti, Resonance, Alia*)

INDIA

On 17 October **Pradeep Behera**, a senior journalist with the English-language *Arunchal Times*, was seriously assaulted by six armed men at his home in the northeast. The attack was apparently related to critical articles Behera had written on social issues. (RSF)

The daily *Amar Asom* reported on 23 October that two of its journalists had been threatened with death by a former separatist militant after they had inquired about his involvement with the police in an attack on a local businessman. (RSF)

On 26 October the Assamese police foiled a murder attempt by militants against **D.N. Bezbouah**, editor of the English-language daily *Sentinel*. Police arrested two suspected members of the United Liberation Front of Assam after finding 'incriminating documents' near Besbouah's home. The two suspects were said to have been planning to assassinate several journalists and intellectuals. (RSF)

In early November the central government ended its monopoly on the provision of internet services, promising to allow private service providers to use surplus communications capacity owned by the country's huge railways network, the Power Grid Corporation of India and electricity boards. Foreign firms are to be permitted to own up to 49 per cent of private service provision. (BBC World Service)

On 3 December a dozen activists of the Hindu chauvinist Shiv Sena party attacked a New Delhi screening of *Fire*, **Deepa Mehta**'s film about a love affair between two sisters-in-law. *Fire* was also withdrawn in Mumbai (Bombay) and the western cities of Surat and Pune, after *Shiv Sena* attacks. Mukhtar Abbas Naqvi, the junior information and broadcasting minister, said that he would re-examine the film - which was pased uncut by the censorship board - to see if it should be banned. (*Guardian*, BBC World Service)

Tens of thousands of Christians held a day of protest on 4 December against the 80 violent acts committed against them in the nine months since the Bharatiya Janata Party (BJP) came to power last March. Virtually all the attacks - which have included the gang rape of nuns, the destruction of churches and the burning of bibles - have been attributed to allies of the BJP, especially the extremist *Vishwa Hindu Parishad* (World Hindu Council). (*Guardian*, BBC World Service)

Recent Publication: *India: Submission to the Advisory Committee established to review provisions of the Protection of Human Rights Act 1993* (AI,

October 1998, 22 pp).

INDONESIA

Human rights volunteer **Martadinata Haryono**, who worked at Volunteer Team for Humanity documenting allegations of rape against ethnic-Chinese women, was murdered on 9 October after the authorities failed to act on repeated threats against her. (AI)

About 15,000 East Timorese took to the streets of Dili on 12 October demanding the resignation of the Indonesian-appointed governor Jose Abiho Soares, who had insisted that all civil servants sign statements supporting Jakarta's policy or face dismissal. (*Guardian*)

On 10 November Canadian journalist **John Stackhouse** was detained by immigration officials at Kuala Lumpur airport and denied permission to enter the country, despite having previously obtained a visa from the Indonesian embassy in New Delhi. Officials told the Canadian embassy that Stackhouse had been temporarily blacklisted following a series of articles he had written on East Timor in 1997. (CC PJ)

On 11 November four journalists - **Saptono** of Antara News Agency, **Eddi Hasby** and **Bambang Wisudo** of *Kompas* magazine and **Tatan Agus** of *Gatra* magazine - were attacked and beaten by security forces whilst covering clashes between soldiers and student demonstrators in Jakarta. Two days afterwards three more

journalists - **Dadang Rhs** of*DeTAk*, **Cosmas Gramiarto** of *Indosiar* and **Yasmin Muntasa** of *ANteve* - were also attacked by security personnel while exercising their profession *(Index 4/1998)*. (CPJ) (IFJ)

On 16 November police questioned 10 opposition politicians suspected of 'instigating the people's movement' and arrested **Sri Bintang Pamungkas** (*Index 3/1997, 4/1997*) for incitement although he claimed he had been 'trying to use my freedom to speak about the need for reform'. (*Guardian*)

IRAN

Tous editor **Mashallah Shamsol-va-Ezine**, sub-editor **Mohammed Javadi-Hessar** and journalist **Ebrahim Nabavi**, who were arrested on 16 September (*Index 6/1998*), were released on 22 October although they remain accused of 'subversion' and may face trial by Islamic court and a possible death penalty. (RSF)

As a response to the commencement on 30 October of CIA-funded Radio Free Europe/Liberty (RFE/RL) broadcasts from Czech soil, Tehran has recalled Ambassador Jafar Hashemi who called the transmissions 'an act of aggression'. RFE/RL President Thomas Dine said the Iranian government had obviously not listened to the content or tone of the transmissions, which are balanced and have included the government's criticisms of the service. (*Prague Post*)

Student rallies on 2 November commemorating the 1979 takeover of the US embassy did not include the traditional burning of the US flag and included welcoming invitations to the ex-hostages. (MEI, *Guardian*)

Following his sacking for comments critical of the Republic, the theologian **Mohsen Sa'id Zaada** has had his religious uniform confiscated by the government. The daily *Aiya* reported on 6 November that Sa'id, whose book 'The Rights of Women in the Islamic Era' was banned in September, received this latest ruling in a closed court without access to his lawyer. (*Al-Quds al-'Arabi*)

In October the Khordad-15 Foundation added $300,000 to the $2.5 million bounty on **Salman Rushdie**, despite the ending of the state *fatwa* (*Index* 6/1998). The Rushdie Defence Committee said the rewards are 'designed to galvanise the minority hard-liners.' (*Guardian*)

On 13 November it was reported that the film *Banu*, which had been banned for eight years, has been approved for screening. Director **Dariush Mehrjui** says no one knows why it was banned. 'You never know how a film will be received. For years I have been censoring myself and it makes you crazy.' (*Guardian*)

On 24 November the translator and author **Majid Sharif** was found dead, having left home four days earlier with the intention of

either walking in the mountains or going on pilgrimage to Mashad. A key member of the Committee for Research into the books of Dr Shariati, a Sorbonne-educated lecturer whose banned books advocated the separation of religion and state, Sharif had published widely on the same topic, notably for the journal *Iran Farda* (Iran Tomorrow). His body showed no signs of violence. (Writers in Prison Committee, PEN)

On 22 November veteran opposition leader **Dariush Forouhar** and his wife **Parvaneh** were discovered dead in their flat, having been stabbed by unknown assailants. Forouhar had served as Labour Minister in Iran's first government after the 1979 Islamic revolution, and later became leader of the illegal but tolerated Iran Nation Party, which published a newsletter often carrying reports of alleged human rights violations. On 26 November the couple's funeral in Tehran turned into a nationalist rally with some of the tens of thousands of mourners chanting liberation slogans and praising the late leftist-nationalist Mohammed Mossadegh who had helped inspire Forouhar and his party. On the same day President Khatami delivered a strong speech to officials at the Intelligence Ministry saying the killers must be brought to justice. The police have arrested a number of people in the case. (*International Herald Tribune, Guardian*)

In its 28 November edition, the newspaper *Kar e Karagar* reported rumours of the

'execution' of **Pirouz Davani**, a leftist politician and editor-in-chief of the newspaper *Pirouz*, who disappeared at the end of August. (RSF)

On 7 December it was reported that '**Azza Allah Sahabi,** director of *Iran Fordha* (Iran Tomorrow), had been ordered by a court 'to stop all [journalistic] activities' for one year and to pay a fine of US$1,000, for having published a caricature critical of the army. The paper is close to the banned yet tolerated Iranian Liberation Movement, and the censoring of its director highlights the growing pressure on the liberal and reformist press. (*Al-Quds al-'Arabi*)

On 9 December the body of poet, writer and free expression advocate **Mohamad Mokhtari** was found in the Tehran city morgue, with marks to his head and neck which suggested he had been strangled. He was last seen alive six days earlier while out shopping. Mokhtari had been arrested several times by the security forces, most recently in October when, with five other writers, he had attempted to found a new writers' association, *Kanoun*. (RSF, HRW)

The body of writer and French translator **Mohammad Ja'frar Pouyandeh**, who disappeared on 9 December, was discovered beneath a railway bridge in a Tehran suburb two days, having apparently been strangled. He had been one of the six dissident writers, along with **Mohamad Mokhtari**, who sought to create an alternative writers' association. Three other writers in the initiative, **Kazem Kordawani**, **Ali Ashraf Darwishian** and **Mansour Koushan**, now fear for their own safety. (Writers in Prison Committee, PEN)

IRAQ

The US-sponsored Radio Free Iraq began broadcasting on 30 October from the Czech Republic. (RFE/RL)

IRELAND

On 27 November the Special Criminal Court in Dublin sentenced the first member of the gang that murdered investigative journalist Veronica Guerin. Paul Ward was sentenced to life imprisonment for his part in Guerin's murder in June 1996 (*Index* 4/96). Groups in Ireland expressed concern at Ward's conviction because it was gained purely on the evidence of the so called 'supergrass' Charlie Bowden a former gang member. (Irish Independent, Guardian)

JORDAN

In September and October 13 members of *Hizb al-Tahrir* (Liberation Party) were sentenced to up to 18 months' imprisonment on charges of membership of illegal associations and distribution of leaflets. (AI)

The list of prohibited subjects under the new Press and Publications law, passed in September, has been increased to include articles that defame the judiciary or instigate unauthorised strikes, sit-ins or public assemblies. Foreign publications must be submitted to the ministry of information prior to distribution and manuscripts are to be vetted by the same body prior to printing in Jordan. Research institutes and public opinion polling centres are forbidden from receiving financial aid from private donors without prior approval. The courts may suspend the publication of any newspaper while a case against it is in progress. However, Prime Minister Fayez Tarawneh has said it is not the government's intention to apply the law strictly. On 17 October the Attorney-General dropped 21 cases and eight pending cases against journalists. (AI)

KAZAKHSTAN

Former Prime Minister **Akezhan Kazhegeldin**, a leading opposition candidate for the 10 January 1999 presidential elections, had his passport confiscated by National Security Committee authorities at Almaty airport as he attempted to board a Lufthansa plane bound for Germany on 27 October. Officers returned Kazhegeldin's passport when they learned that they were being videotaped. Kazhegeldin's campaign, like those of several other candidates, was derailed by his inability to have the judiciary quash a conviction against him for participating in 'a mass gathering by an unsanctioned organisation' in early October. On 24 November the Supreme Court declined to overturn his conviction. Kazhegeldin dubbed it a 'black day for Kazakh democracy'. (RFE/RL, Interfax)

Petr Svoik, co-chairman of the opposition group Azamat, was arrested by Interior Ministry troops on 30 October, and charged with slander, inciting 'national conflict' and insulting an official. Svoik had earlier been charged along with environmental campaigner **Mels Eleusizov** and two others with holding an unauthorised meeting on 2 October of the organisation For Fair Elections in Kyrgyzstan. Eleusizov, head of Tabiyghat, the Kazakh Green party, was given a three-day prison sentence on these charges, and was therefore barred as a presidential candidate. In April 1998, Svoik defended Kazakh Workers Movement (KWM) leader Madel Ismailov during a court appearance for 'insulting the honour and dignity of the president' (*Index* 3/1998). (RFE/RL, AI)

Marat Ospanov, speaker of the lower chamber of parliament, interrupted deputy **Valerii Zemlyanov** on 12 November when the latter tried to suggest that the presidential elections scheduled for 10 January would not be free and fair. Zemlyanov's microphone was then switched off and other deputies began reviling him as an 'obstacle to parliament's work'. (RFE/RL)

Appearing live on KTK-TV on 15 November, presidential candidate and former Customs Committee chairman Gany

Kasymov hurled a vase of flowers at a journalist who reminded him he had earlier vowed never to run against Nazarbayev for the presidency. (RFE/RL)

In court on 24 November opposition leader **Akezhan Kazhegeldin** observed that, since the election was announced in 8 October, six unnamed independent newspapers had been closed. Officials visited many independent media offices during November, warning publishers against covering opposition candidates or publishing negative stories about President Nursultan Nazarbayev, his policies or family. One independent radio station has been told that political stories must be cleared by an 'adviser' before airing; the director of an independent television station told his news department to consider themselves part of the 'president's team'. (International Press Institute, RFE/RL)

Dariga Nazarbayeva, daughter of President Nazarbayev, announced on 6 November that she would temporarily step down as head of the national news agency, Khabar. Nazarbayeva said she made the decision for 'ethical reasons' but that she would resume her duties after the 10 January elections. (RFE/RL)

Almaty City Court ordered the opposition newspaper *DAT* to close because of bankruptcy on 2 December. The court appointed a commission to liquidate the newspaper's assets, warning its owners to stop publishing, or

face further prosecution. The case against *DAT* on charges of unpaid taxes was opened in the summer of 1998. Tax officials seized some of the newspaper's assets, but *DAT* had issues published abroad and transported to Kazakhstan. Customs officials have impounded the copies several times, most recently with the 31 October issue. The seizure followed a 28 October article detailing the overseas assets of President Nursultan Nazarbayev. *DAT* illustrated the article with a picture of a villa in Saint-Tropez, France, said to be owned by Nazarbayev and worth US$119 million. (RFE/RL)

KENYA

The managing director of the *Star* newspaper, **Francis Mathenge Wanderi**, and editor-in-chief **Magayu Kiarie Magayu** were released on 13 October after their prosecution for issuing an 'alarming publication' was dismissed by a Nairobi court (*Index* 5/1998) . The prosecution had alleged that an article entitled 'The Shoddy Deals Grounding AT&H [African Tours and Hotels]' was likely to cause 'fear'. (Ndima)

On 17 October cabinet minister Sharrif Nassir warned that the ruling KANU party would no longer tolerate 'insults from the press'. He accused unnamed newspapers and magazines of 'specialising in hurling insults at President Moi and the government' and warned that their days were numbered. 'We shall set their printing presses on fire [and]

we shall make sure no vendor will touch their papers. He said that the papers which report negatively about the Kanu party will be taught 'a lesson they would never forget'. (Ndima)

East African Standard's editor-in-chief **Kamau Kanyanga** was fired, or 'forced to leave', on 19 October and replaced with former *Weekly Review* editor Wachira Waruru. The *Standard* newspaper group recently acquired Kenya Television Network (KTN), the first privately run station and attempted to put it under receivership, a move blocked by KTN's debtors. It is not clear why Kanyanga was fired, although he was accused of 'running the paper down'. (Media Institute*)*

Nation Media Group columnist **Wahome Mutahi** was told by his editors in late October that the paper would no longer publish his articles if he continued to write humorous open letters to President Daniel arap Moi. Mutahi writes the popular 'Whispers' column. (Media Institute, NDIMA)

East.African Standard's chief parliamentary reporter **David Okwembah** had his press pass impounded on 28 October on orders of the national assembly clerk, David Masya, barring him from covering debate in parliament. However, temporary Deputy Speaker Gitobu Imanyara ordered on October 29 the reinstatement of the impounded pass. 'As long as I am in this chair, the *Standard*'s chief parliamentary reporter will be allowed in the house, until the speaker makes a ruling', Imanyara said. (*Daily Nation*)

A ban on opposition leader **Kenneth Matiba**'s book, *Kenya: Return to Reason* (*Index* 3/1994) was lifted on 15 November, nearly five years after the ban was imposed. The court of appeal ruled that the book contained 'a concise record of Kenya's political, economic, and human rights history...' (Ndima, *Daily Nation*)

Recent publication: Steeves, H. Leslie, 1998: *Gender Violence and the Press: The St Kizito Story* (Ohio University Press, 176 pp)

Throup David, 1998 : *Multiparty Politics in Kenya: The Kenyatta and Moi States and the Triumph of the System in the 1992 Election* (Ohio University Press, 290 pp).

KYRGYZSTAN

The Human Rights Committee of Kyrgyzstan (HRCK) announced on 2 October that the justice ministry had forced it to close, following the discovery of 'procedural irregularities' in its 1996 registration. Two founding members, whose names were included in its charter, apparently did not attend the HRCK's founding conference. (*Turkistan Newsletter*, RFE/RL)

The justice ministry filed a petition in Bishkek on 15 October, asking for the closure of the *Paishamba*, *Limon* and *Kaptama-Digest* publications on the grounds that they were primarily pornographic. *Limon*'s owner,

Marat Tazabekov, who is honorary Canadian consul to Kyrgyzstan, later reached an agreement with the ministry to cease publishing the alleged pornography, as did *Paishamba*'s owner, **Shailoobek Duisheev**, who is also deputy chief editor of the weekly *Asaba*. Duisheev said *Paishamba* would be closed on 31 December 1998 and be replaced by a new paper, *Juuchu*, from 1 January 1999. (*Turkistan Newsletter*)

Omurbek Subanaliev, security head for the Osh region, called off a 21 October news conference at which he had been scheduled to detail his office's 9 October seizure of 700 tonnes of Iranian weapons, in transit to northern Afghanistan as 'humanitarian aid'. He told the meeting that National Security Minister Misir Ashirkulov had persuaded him not to answer questions. The 17 railway cars had previously transited Turkmen and Uzbek territories without incident. In reward for his attention to duty, Subanaliev was dismissed from his job on 26 October. (*Turkistan Newsletter*)

The chairman of the Erkin Kyrgyzstan opposition party, **Topchubek Turgunaliev**, was released from prison on 24 November. Turgunaliev was sent to prison for four years on charges of abuse of power in February 1997, after earlier charges of embezzlement and forgery were dropped. The charges stemmed from the period when Turgunaliev was rector at the Bishkek University of Humanities in 1994. (RFE/RL)

LESOTHO

On 3 November **Naleli Ntlamahad**, a regular columnists with the *Public Eye* newspaper, had his house broken into by South African National Defence Force soldiers, ostensibly in the country on a peace-keeping mission. They arrived in two armoured cars, broke in to the house and ransacked it for two hours. The journalist, who was not at home, believes he was harassed because of articles critical of the presence of South African troops. (MISA)

On 10 November the office of the independent weekly newspaper *MoAfrika* was broken into. Senior reporter **Rabuka Chatse** arrived at the office to begin the day's work and found doors and desk drawers wide open. The intruders stole US$510 and advertisers 'cheques totalling US$650 from the cash deposit box. (MISA)

LIBERIA

On 14 October the ministry of information announced a ban on posting any information on the Internet. The order stated the media were operating online news agencies without permit and 'running unauthenticated newspaper articles and gossip columns'. (CPJ)

The ministry of posts and telecommunications on 23 October withdrew the shortwave frequencies assigned to the independent Star Radio. A statement said the decision was based on a recent decision to review all shortwave broadcasting stations. Star Radio, which is funded by the US Agency for International Aid, provides independent information on civic and local concerns. (CPJ)

On 28 October Star Radio's administrator **Dr Jeanette Carter** and station manager **George Bennet** were ordered by the ministry of labour to cease working because, as foreign nationals, they were illegally employed. They were also threatened with deportation unless they paid fines amounting to US$2,000. (CPJ)

MACEDONIA

On 1 November the Bulgarian ambassador Angel Dimitrov protested at the state's refusal to allow two Bulgarian journalists to enter the country to cover the the second round of the general elections. **Marinela Mircheva**, a state radio radio journalist, and **Antoaneta Maskrachka** of 24 Chasa were denied entry despite having the necessary accreditation. Bulgarian media have reported that Prime Minister Branco Crvenkovski is 'waging a wild, anti-Bulgarian campaign'. (RFE/RL)

On 17 November Greek journalist **Thodoros Varikos** was detained during the trial against Nikolas Konstantinidis, for taking notes. (Greek Helsinki Monitor)

MALAYSIA

At least 232 people were arrested for illegal assembly, and more were beaten when police used force to break up a peaceful demonstration in Kuala Lumpur on 24 October. The same day police gave participants of a forum convened to discuss the repeal of the Internal Security Act 10 minutes to leave the building, or face arrest. (AI)

A 1997 Malaysian Special Branch report to Prime Minister Mahathir Mohamad, released on 6 November, revealed that the sexual allegations against **Anwar Ibrahim** were 'baseless' and that he had been the victim of a smear campaign (*Index* 6/1998). The credibility of the prosecution's case was further damaged when Mohamad Said Awang, Special Branch chief, admitted he might lie to the court if told to do so by government ministers. (*Guardian*)

US Vice-President Al Gore outraged his hosts at the Asian-Pacific Economic Co-operation summit on 16 November when he extolled the virtues of Asian pro-democracy movements and quoted reform slogans in a banquet speech. On 23 November the foreign ministry summoned the US ambassador to reiterate its view on that Gore's speech was 'an incitement of lawlessness and not simply a call of democracy as claimed'. (*Guardian, Star Online*)

Anwar Ibrahim's defence lawyer, **Zainur Zakaria**, was sentenced to three months imprisonment for contempt of court on 30 November, after submitting an affidavit from his client which alleged that two prosecutors had tried to persuade a friend of Ibrahim's to implicate him falsely in illegal sex acts. The judge ruled that the affidavit was 'an interference with the course of justice'. (*Guardian*)

MEXICO

Jesús Blancornelas, columnist for the investigative magazine *Zeta*, received on 22 October the Columbia University Press Award, given to reporters who have contributed to Inter-American press freedom. Blancornelas has investigated cocaine trafficking to the US. (Freedom Forum)

Claudio Cortés García, a journalist with the Mexican edition of *Le Monde Diplomatique*, was found dead in the back seat of a vehicle in Mexico City on 23 October. He had disappeared on the night of 20 October. Preliminary investigations by the attorney-general's office indicated that he had been strangled over 10 hours prior to the discovery of his body. García, the son of a former political prisoner, also worked for the dailies *Reforma* and *El Financiero*, and the magazine *La Crisis*. The Mexican edition of *Le Monde Diplomatique* was suspended in the mid-1980s after its then director, **Ivan Meléndez**, was murdered. Publication was resumed last year. (RSF, CPJ, *Guardian*)

On 29 October **Pedro Valle Fernández**, a state radio and television reporter, was shot to death while sitting in his car. He had recently produced a report exposing a local child-prostitution ring. (RSF)

NAMIBIA

Gwen Lister, editor of the *Namibian* newspaper, on 12 October expressed concern at accusations by supporters of the ruling SWAPO party that the independent press had an 'anti-government agenda'. (MISA)

Home Affairs Minister Jerry Ekandjo said on 6 November that his ministry will draft controversial anti-homosexuality legislation. He told parliament that the planned legislation would introduce heavy penalties against lesbians and gays and that it would curb the spread of homosexual practices. (e-mail from Romanzo Steenkamp)

A South African Broadcasting Corporation (SABC) TV crew, was briefly detained on 24 November in the Caprivi Strip while reporting on political tension in the area. It was the second crew to be detained in less than a week. The two crew members, journalists **Jessica Pitchford** and cameraman **Dudley Saunders**, were held by security forces after they apparently strayed into a restricted area. Earlier in the week, two more SABC journalists, **Montlenyane Diphoko** and **Thabo Modise**, had been detained and their video footage and equipment were seized. They were released a day later following intervention from South Africa's deputy president, Thabo Mbeki. They were told that the footage was being scrutinised for possible censorship, in case

it contained material reflecting negatively on the government. (MISA)

Fred Simasiku, a reporter with the state-owned *New Era* newspaper, has been suspended by the acting Permanent Secretary of the Information and Broadcasting Ministry, James Sankwasa, for alleging that Sankwasa had been aware of the political turmoil in the Caprivi region which is threatening secession. Sankwasa, who is also managing director of *New Era*, initially sued his own paper for defamation. (MISA)

NIGER

On 27 October **Ibrahim Hanidou**, chief editor of the weekly *La Tribune du Peuple*, and **Abdul Mounime Ousseyni**, chief editor of *Citoyen* weekly, each received a six-month suspended sentence for defamation in a Niamey court. This sentence followed the filing of a complaint by the consul of Niger in Jeddah, Saudi Arabia, whom the newspapers had accused of being implicated in passport trafficking. *La Tribune du Peuple* and *Citoyen* were ordered to pay fines of US$180 and US$5,400 respectively in damages and interest. The following day, Daula Diallo, president of the Superior Council on Communications, announced that, from 31 October, all newspapers whose chief editors were not holders of professional journalists' licences would be suspended. He also forbade private radio stations relaying foreign reports during their news programmes. (RSF)

It was reported on 28 October that *Le Républicain, Tribune du Peuple, La Bonne Affaire, Le Citoyen, Sahel Horizon* and *Sankore* newspapers had been threatened with closure by the Conseil Supérieur de la Communication, as have the radio stations Anafani and RM. (IFJ)

NIGERIA

Baguada Kaltho, Kaduna State senior correspondent of the *News, Tempo* and *PMNews*, has been reported missing by his employers, Independent Communication Network Limited. He disappeared in March 1996. On 18 August, 1998, police said Kaltho had been killed in a bomb blast on 18 January 1996. They said he was trying to throw the bomb at the Durbar Hotel in Kaduna, a claim contested by the journalists family, media and human rights organisations. ('IPR')

The wife of **Niran Malaolu**, the imprisoned editor of the *Diet* newspaper (Index 2/1998, 3/1998, 4/1998, 5/1998), has raised alarm over her husband's health in prison. In a late October appeal sent to head of state General Abdulsalam Abubakar, Bukola Malaolu said prison authorities had not allowed him to receive medical treatment for typhoid fever and that he had a permanent headache. ('IPR')

On 17 November the Lagos Federal High Court granted damages of US$32,294 to Arit and Obosa Igiebor, wife and five-year old daughter of *Tell* magazine's editor-in-chief, **Nosa Igiebor** for trauma inflicted on them during a raid on their residence in September 1997 by State Security Services (SSS) agents (*Index* 6/1997). They pointed a loaded gun at the head of the then three-year-old Obosa, demanding that her mother tell them where her father was. (CPJ)

PAKISTAN

On 2 October **Abdul Hafiz Hamid Azizi**, an Afghan journalist based in Peshawar who works for the newspapers *Sahaar* and *Wahdat*, was shot and wounded by two Afghans.

On 6 October **Najeeda Sara Bibi,** an Afghan journalist employed by the BBC World Service, was shot at but not injured by unidentified assailants while shopping in a Peshawar market. Both journalists have angered the Taliban and local Islamic fundamentalists with their reporting. (RSF)

Lakhano Siyal, a senior journalist, was found murdered on 18 October. Siyal was the former vice-president of the Hyderabad Press Club and ex-chief reporter for the dailies *Aftab* and *Ibrat*. He also worked for the Sindhi daily *Mehran*. Police have arrested 13 persons on suspicion. (Pakistan Press Foundation)

On 21 October the office of the daily *Post International* and the fortnightly *Badbaan* were ransacked by unidentified assailants. **Sohail Rana**, chief editor of both newspapers, alleged that the senior superintendent of police in Islamabad and the local station house officer masterminded

the attack on the office as a punishment for publishing a story on the escalating crime rate in the city. (Pakistan Press Foundation, *Muslim*)

In the run-up to an impending battle with the Senate over his move to replace British common law with Islamic teachings (*Index* 6/1998), Prime Minister Nawaz Sharif called on 17 November for the introduction of Taliban-style rapid Islamic justice. He reportedly told a rally that 'crimes have virtually come to naught' in Afghanistan and 'one can safely drive a vehicle [there] full of gold at midnight'. (Reuters, AI)

On 23 November it was reported that **Abdul Rasul**, a Muslim activist from the Chinese province of Xinjiang, had been detained by police for failing to obtain permission for a news conference in Islamabad. Rasul was trying to draw attention to the condition of Muslims in Xinjiang. Police sources said that he would not be charged. (BBC World Service)

Recent Publication: *No progress on women's rights* (AI, September 1998, 22 pp)

PALESTINE (AUTONOMOUS AREAS)

On 8 October **Hossam Abou Alan**, an AFP photograper, was shot in the back of the neck by Israeli soldiers while covering a Palestinian demonstration in Hebron which developed into a skirmish with Jewish settlers. He is the tenth journalist to

have been shot this year by troops. The danger was highlighted again on 10 October when **Amira Hass**, reporting for *Haíaretz* in a village south of Nablus, was shot at with a rifle from the nearby settlement of Yitzhar. (RSF)

PANAMA

On 24 November **Gustavo Gorriti** of *La Prensa* magazine was awarded one of the five prizes for investigative journalism by the organisation Committee to Protect Journalists. (CPJ).

PERU

On 11 October, just after the municipal elections, Mayor Enrique Gutierrez of Camaná and a group of supporters burst in and sacked the offices of the radio station Radio Armonía. The director of the radio station, **Alfredo del Carpio Linares**, who complained that the police did nothing to stop the attack, has been threatened with death and told to leave the city within a week. (IPYS)

Journalist **Roxana Torricelli Farfán** and photographer **Lorenzo Ayasta Tenorio** were attacked by shop owners in the Aguas Verdes shopping centre on 21 October for reporting on the presence of contraband goods in the market. (IPYS)

On 21 October the mayor of the Satipo province announced that he would initiate legal action against journalist **Santos Rojas**, director and host of the news programme 'Press Freedom'

• •

HOSSAM ABOU ALAN
'I fell on my camera'

'I was filming a boy who was hit by a rubber bullet in Bab al-Zawieh in Hebron when an Israeli military policeman fired another, hitting me in the back of the head. I fell on my camera and my face was badly wounded. I was immediately taken to Alia hospital in Hebron, then transferred to the emergency room at al-Ahli. The bullet entered through my skull and caused a great deal of damage. I was operated on for three and a half hours, and the surgery was a success. I am still in hospital.

I found out that a sniper standing at a street corner fired the bullet. He had a Hebrew newspaper. We had seen him before shooting citizens, and then pretending to read the paper. He is a military policeman. We spoke with a group of soldiers from Nahal unit three days prior to my injury. They said they hated it when we are around because they could not do their job well. This is why I believe that I was deliberately shot. One could easily figure out I was a reporter. I was wearing a flack jacket and carrying my camera. I was standing with colleagues who were also carrying cameras. The distance between the soldiers and me was very short. They could clearly tell that we were reporters. This is not the first time we were shot at deliberately. I was shot several times before, and Israeli soldiers and settlers also beat me up. My equipment was destroyed many times.

I am still suffering from my wound. I have bad headaches and severe pain in my spinal column. I am always exhausted. The doctors gave me medicine to take every day for a period of two years. I want to go back to work some day. I will not give up my job no matter what. Many of my friends suffered worse injuries than myself. They were determined to return to work and they did. I am still alive with my wife and kids. That is all that matters.' ❑

Hossam Abou Alan is a photographer with Agence France Presse

• •

on radio Studio 99. Rojas has criticised irregularities in the local administration. (IPYS)

On 26 October the Cecilia Valencuela's television news programme 'Without Censorship' was unexpectedly cancelled. She had received a death threat a week earlier in an envelope bearing the seal of Congress. The letter, composed of newspaper clippings, read: 'You're going to die, bitch'. (CPJ)

Augusto Norena Llanos, director of the regional newspaper *Diario Regional*, received telephone death threats on 28 and 29 October. An anonymous voice told him to stop criticising the management of the mayor of the Huanuco region, Luzmina Templo Condeso. The journalist has been stalked since publicising irregularities committed by the regional authorities. (Asociaçion Naçional de Periodistas)

On 2 November two phone calls were made threatening journalist **Gustavo Mohme Llona** from the Lima daily *La Republica* with death if he covered the visit of members of the Inter-American Commission on Human Rights (IACHR) that arrived that week. (CPJ)

On 9 November media proprietor **Baruch Ivcher** said that he had received death threats for a week because of the IACHR's visit. It was triggered by his complaining that he had his citizenship and shares in Frecuencia Latina/Channel 2 television station had been taken away (*Index* 4/1997, 5/1997,

6/1997, 2/1998, 3/1998, 4/1998, 5/1998, 6/1998). (IPYS)

On 9 November an unknown person assaulted and threatened journalist **Bacario Alejandro Bautista Yucra**, correspondent of Lima-based radio station Radio Union and host of the news programme *Contacto A* on Radio Studio A. Bautista had carried a series about local drug and delinquency problems. A few days before the attack he had broadcast a report on drugs and violence in the Palpa region. (IPYS)

On 12 November the news director of the Radiodifusora Sudamericana station, **Romulo Ripa Casafranca**, was victim of a violent attack when two assailants broke into his office. The assault followed numerous threats by the head of the Andahuaylas district, Vicente Zegarra Suarez, who had previously tried to bribe the journalist without success. Ripa had been reporting on the abuse of the local authorities of local farmers as well as on the mismanagement of funds destined to fight the effects of El Niño. Two colleagues of Ripa, **Alipio Cancho Alana** and **Carlos Arévalo**, had also been threatened on 17 November after complaining to the Ombudsman about Ripa's assault. (IPYS).

Paul Garay Ramírez, editor-in-chief of the *Quincenario del Pueblo* was attacked while riding a motorcycle on 13 November. The attacker was identified as Walter Ortiz Meza, leader of the Pucallpa municipal

worker's union. The journalist has been reporting on mismanagement and corruption cases involving government officials. (IPYS)

On 1 December a campaign aimed at discrediting journalists was launched on the internet. Opposition politicians and journalists critical of the government appear in a black list, among them **Cesar Hildebrandt**, **Cecilia Valenzuela**, **Fernando Rospigliosi**, **Manuel D'Ornellas** and **Miguel Angel Páez**. The site, regularly updated, is run by the Association for the Defence of the Truth, registered in Miami. (IPYS)

RUSSIA

On 26 October the Duma instructed its Security Committee to investigate the claim by parliamentary deputy and Communist Party member Igor Bratischev that President Boris Yeltsin had been clinically dead for 17 minutes on 15 October. Bratischev cited a report in the *Novii Petersburg* newspaper. (RFE/RL)

RWANDA

Emmanuel Bagambiki, a detainee at the International Tribunal Court in Arusha, refused to plead at his initial court appearance on 10 November and complained that he had not been allowed to engage a defence lawyer of his choice. Bagambiki, a former prefect of Cyangugu, said he had no confidence in the Belgian lawyer assigned him by the tribunal. (IRIN, Hirondelle News Agency)

• •

SERGEI KOVALEV
Murder incorporated

L ike everyone with any sense, I believe the murder of Galina Starovoitova was a politically motivated contract killing. And, like innumerable crimes of the same kind, I do not think it will ever be solved. Starovoitova's death is symptomatic of the political evolution of our country. Russia today is at a dangerous crossroad in its history. I see no possible way forward for the democrats and I am all too aware of the deplorable state of our society. We set out to create a civil society, but we have not gone far in that direction.

Powerful political forces like the Communist Party (KPRF) and the patriot-nationalists are exploiting the present tragic situation. They are asking for the introduction of a state of emergency and increasing their attacks on the press. You will see the united front between the communists and the 'law and order' brigade taking shape from now on.

The composition of the present government is an obvious sign of the danger I mentioned above. Who is Evgeni Primakov [prime minister and formerly a senior officer in the KGB], who is Yuri Masliukov [first deputy prime minister, a communist and former head of Gosplan], what is their past? You could ask the same questions about many other ministers. These people made their careers in the Soviet system; they have not changed and have learned little. Even Boris Yeltsin has demonstrated that he is a past master in the old communist methods.

And there is another sign: pressure on the media is growing and, unfortunately, is succeeding all too easily. For instance, I have been banned from ORT [Russia's leading TV channel]. The press is officially free but it is the victim of political pressure and of the oligarchs who own and control it. Its dependency has become an important political factor. Meanwhile, the communists are calling for a committee for 'control and vigilance'.

I don't think the Communist Party is actually growing in numbers, but the communists are running a hideously effective propaganda campaign, distinguished by its gross lies about the policies of the reformers, among the vast number of disaffected people in our society. In effect, they are gathering a protest vote. Let me give you an example: when they say they are not anti-semitic they are lying. Anti-semitism has been a strand in state policy

• •

for decades. Only fools refuse to see it. The anti-semitic outburst of the communist deputy Albert Makachov – an evil brute – wouldn't worry me if it wasn't for the fact that he is simply articulating what Gennadi Zouganov [leader of the KPRF] actually thinks. What really terrifies me is that the Duma refused to condemn one of its members.

The lack of unity among the democratic forces is a problem. Despite all the attempts at unity they remain tragically fragmented. In 1994 and 1995 I was alone in calling for unity; now I fear that once again personal ambitions will overcome democratic responsibilities.

Our 'democracy' is only a good as its 'democrats'. In 1996, Anatoli Choubaïs [former leader of the 'young reformers' when they were part of the government] organised the re-election of Boris Yeltsin on the orders of our oligarchs and with their money. It was a criminal error on his part. As a result, we have a strange puppet-like figure rather than a president.

The reformers, backed by the West, have gambled on Yeltsin and lost. The West's responsibility is huge in other repects too. Bill Clinton and Helmut Kohl, for instance, had the political means to end the war in Chechnya. But they refused to act, believing that Yeltsin was the only guarantee of democracy. My great friend Andrei Sakharov once said: 'My country needs support, but also pressure.' Because of its own hypocrisy and cowardice the West has always feared to exert that pressure. ❏

Galina Starovoitova, a deputy in the Russian Duma, was assassinated outside her St Petersburg home on 20 November. **Sergei Kovalev** *was, at one time, Boris Yeltsin's commissioner for human rights. He continues to be an activist in this field. He was interviewed by François Bonnet for* Le Monde. *Translation by JVH.*

Recent Publication: Gourevitch, Philip, 1998: *We Wish to Inform You That Tomorrow We Will Be Killed With Our Families: Stories From Rwanda* (Farrar Strauss & Giroux, 384 pp); *Rwanda: Insurgency in north-western Rwanda,* (November 1998, Africa Rights); Howard Adelman and Astri Suhrke, 1999: *The Path of a Genocide: The Rwanda Crisis from Uganda to Zaire* (Transaction Publications)

SERBIA-MONTENGRO

On 13 October the Belgrade dailies *Danas* and *Dnevni Telegraf* were served with banning orders. The information ministry said the ban and seizure of the paper's equipment was a temporary measure, lasting only while the government's emergency decree on media remained in force (*Index* 6/1998). Similar measures were announced against a third independent daily, *Nasa Borba,* but no action was taken. All three were accused of 'inciting fear, panic and defeatism'. (ANEM, B92, RSF)

On 19 October the state news agency Tanjug announced that two of its employees, journalist **Nebojsa Radosevic** and photographer **Vladimir Dobricic**, had gone missing on the Prishtina-Magura road in Kosovo, the second journalist abduction since the conflict began. On 1 November the Kosova Liberation Army said a guerrilla 'military court' had sentenced the two journalists to 60 days' imprisonment for 'violation and disregard of rules on civilian and military

organisation'. (AMARC, RFE/RL)

On 20 October the Serbian parliament adopted a new Law on Public Information. A media outlet will henceforth be deemed guilty as soon as the state charges it with a 'misdemeanour' and it will be punishable by enormous fines and ruthless trial procedures. A ban was imposed on listening to foreign radio stations. (AMARC, ANEM)

On 23 October, **Slavko Curuvija**, owner and chief executive of the magazine *Evropljanin,* was summoned to a hearing at the Court of Law for Offences under the pretext that several articles and illustrations in the last issue of the magazine violated article 67 of the new information act. Found guilty of several misdemeanours, including 'publishing innacurate information' in a number of photographs, illustrations and texts of the October issue, **Curuvija** was fined a maximum 800 thousand dinars (US$80,000) under the guidelines of the new law. **Dragan Bujosevic** and **Ivan Tadic** were also ordered to pay 400 thousand dinars each, while the DeTe Press company, which publishes *Evropljanin,* was fined 800 thousand dinars. All payments were due within 24 hours. Curuvija was expected to file an appeal. All three journalists suffered further harassment on 26 October when their passports were seized by the authorities. They were also denied one-third of their salaries which, according to the Belgrade municipal court baliff, would be withheld until

they are acquitted. (AMARC, ANEM)

On 28 October criminal charges were brought against **Nenad Cekic**, editor of Radio Index, for unauthorised use of the radio station. The charges came after it was evicted from its premises by the telecommunications ministry, and taken off the transmitter it had used despite having a valid contract with State Radio Television Serbia. The case followed similar shutdowns for City Radio in Nis, Radio Konntakt in Prishtina, RTV Pirot and Radio Senta. On 10 November Cekic was dismissed as editor-in-chief of the station in a move said to have been initiated by Deputy Prime Minister Vojislav Seselj. (ANEM)

On 4 November the independent Belgrade daily *Danas* was due to resume publication after a three week lay-off. According to the paper's editor-in-chief, **Grujica Spasojevic**, it would be published in Montenegro after it was banned under the government's decree on information during the period of threatened NATO air strikes. However, the following day police prevented *Danas* from entering Serbia. The Montenegro Secretary for Information Bozidar Jaredic warned Serbia against any further interference with Montenegran publications. (B92)

On 5 November the editor-in-chief of the Belgrade daily *Dnevni Telegraf,* **Slavko Curuvija**, said the paper could not be published that

Simon Davies on

PRIVACY

Patricia Williams on

RACE

Gabriel Garcia Marquez on

JOURNALISM

Edward Lucie-Smith on

THE INTERNET

Ursula Owen on

...all in INDEX

SUBSCRIBE & SAVE

UK and overseas

○ **Yes! I want to subscribe to *Index*.**

- ❐ 1 year (6 issues) £39 Save 28%
- ❐ 2 years (12 issues) £74 Save 31%
- ❐ 3 years (18 issues) £102 **You save 37%**

Name

Address

B9B1

£ _____ enclosed. ❏ Cheque (£) ❏ Visa/MC ❏ Am Ex ❏ Bill me
(*Outside of the UK, add £6 a year for foreign postage*)

Card No.

Expiry Signature

❏ I do not wish to receive mail from other companies.

INDEX ✉ Freepost: INDEX, 33 Islington High Street, London N1 9BR
☎ (44) 171 278 2313 Fax: (44) 171 278 1878
e tony@indexoncensorship.org

SUBSCRIBE & SAVE

North America

○ **Yes! I want to subscribe to *Index*.**

- ❐ 1 year (6 issues) $52 Save 21%
- ❐ 2 years (12 issues) $96 Save 27%
- ❐ 3 years (18 issues) $135 **You save 32%**

Name

Address

B9B1

$ _____ enclosed. ❏ Cheque ($) ❏ Visa/MC ❏ Am Ex ❏ Bill me

Card No.

Expiry Signature

❏ I do not wish to receive mail from other companies.

✉ INDEX, 708 Third Avenue, 8th Floor, New York, NY 10017
☎ (44) 171 278 2313 Fax: (44) 171 278 1878
e tony@indexoncensorship.org

Simon Davies on

PRIVACY

Patricia Williams on

RACE

Gabriel Garcia Marquez on

JOURNALISM

Edward Lucie-Smith on

THE INTERNET

Ursula Owen on

HATE SPEECH

...all in

SUBSCRIBE & SAVE

UK and overseas

○ **Yes! I want to subscribe to *Index*.**

❒ 1 year (6 issues)	£39	Save 28%
❒ 2 years (12 issues)	£74	Save 31%
❒ 3 years (18 issues)	£102	**You save 37%**

Name

Address

B9B1

£ _____ enclosed. ❑ Cheque (£) ❑ Visa/MC ❑ Am Ex ❑ Bill me
(*Outside of the UK, add £6 a year for foreign postage*)

Card No.

Expiry   Signature

❑ I do not wish to receive mail from other companies.

✉ Freepost: INDEX, 33 Islington High Street, London N1 9BR
☎ (44) 171 278 2313   Fax: (44) 171 278 1878
e tony@indexoncensorship.org

SUBSCRIBE & SAVE

North America

○ **Yes! I want to subscribe to *Index*.**

❒ 1 year (6 issues)	$52	Save 21%
❒ 2 years (12 issues)	$96	Save 27%
❒ 3 years (18 issues)	$135	**You save 32%**

Name

Address

B9B1

$ _____ enclosed. ❑ Cheque ($) ❑ Visa/MC ❑ Am Ex ❑ Bill me

Card No.

Expiry   Signature

❑ I do not wish to receive mail from other companies.

✉ INDEX, 708 Third Avenue, 8th Floor, New York, NY 10017
☎ (44) 171 278 2313   Fax: (44) 171 278 1878
e tony@indexoncensorship.org

day because financial police and tax inspectors had been guarding the printing house used by the paper with the intention of confiscating copies as soon as they were printed. The paper eventually returned to the news stands on 7 November but the owners were again immediately fined for violating the state's new information act. Editor **Dragan Novakovic** and the Montenegran-based firm *Dnevni Telegraf* were obliged to pay roughly US$120,000. The paper was accused of disrupting the Yugoslav and Serbian constitutional orders by publishing an ad from a student organisation in its Saturday edition. The state offensive continued on 9 November when the Public Income Department confiscated all copies of the paper. Curuvija was adamant that this provocation would not result in he or his staff leaving Belgrade, however the possibility remained that it might be published in future in Bulgaria, Hungary, or Italy. Some copies appeared on the streets on 19 November, but distribution was minimal after news stand proprietors were pressured not to handle it. (B92)

On 7 November four students arrested 24 hours earlier were sentenced to 10 days imprisonment for creating a public disturbance and writing anti-government slogans. All were arrested while painting a clenched fist, the symbol of the student resistance movement, on a Belgrade wall. (B92)

On 11 November Belgrade-based independent Radio B92

was presented with the 1998 MTV Free Your Mind award in Milan 'in recognition of its courageous and inspirational coverage of the tragic events in Serbia'. The ceremony was relayed live on TV Kosova, owned by Maria Milosevic, daughter of the Yugoslav president, but it was abruptly interrupted after B92's name was announced. The station broadcast commercials during the acceptance speech of **Veran Matic**, B92's editor-in-chief. (ANEM)

On 13 November **Peter Furst** of the Swiss newspaper *Tages Anzeiger* was denied a visa as he was considered persona non grata because of his coverage of the war and politics in the state. (IFJ)

On 18 November **Sandra Radovanovic**, a journalist for the daily *Glas Javnosti*, was convicted of defaming two Kragujevac lawyers and fined 50,000 dinars (US$5,000).

On 19 November copies of the Podgorica weekly *Monitor*, bound for Serbia, were confiscated near the border. The following day the magazine was fined US$300,000 for printing an ad for the student organisation Otpor. This was the largest fine levied so far under the new Public Information Act. (B92)

On 19 October the government gave an assurance that it had no intention of regulating the ownership of print media or breaking up the four main newspaper groups. The government said

that the setting up of the Media Development Agency was critical to help extend the spread in the base of ownership by allocating resources to media establishments with potential but which were hampered by lack of skills and insufficient advertising. (*Southern Africa Report*)

Student journalist **Max Hamata** was expelled from the Peninsula Technikon on 17 November, following his article on campus sex and prostitution on published in the *Mail and Guardian* last September (*Index* 6/1998). He was expelled by an internal disciplinary committee, though he was not present at the hearing. (FXI)

On 20 November **Layla Cassim**, a pupil at Crawford School, was suspended after a request to her headmaster from the Jewish Defence League to investigate claims that Cassim had placed an article she wrot, that 'reflected' the Palestinian Liberation Organisation's political philosophy, on the school's notice board. A week earlier, a Jewish group threatened to take action against Cassim's Muslim family because of what she wrote in the article, which was her history assignment. (FXI)

On 28 October **Santhalingham Sriganjan**, journalist for the Tamil daily *Virakesari*, was released on bail and told to appear in court when called upon to do so. He was arrested last July on suspicion of having links with the separatist Liberation Tigers of Tamil Eelam (*Index* 5/98, 6/98). (Reuters, *Inform*)

On 11 November the inaugural meeting of the National Alliance for Peace, a broad coalition of peace and social justice activists, was disrupted by members of the Sinhalese chauvinist National Movement Against Terrorism (NMAT). NMAT members yelled for the death of the leader of the Liberation Tigers of Tamil Eelam, Vellupillai Prabhakaran, attempted to forcibly take over the stage and distributed a leaflet calling for the investigation and arrest of journalists whom NMAT believes have disobeyed the ban on contact with the Tigers. (National Peace Council)

Recent Publication: *Internal Flight Alternative: An Update* (Canadian Immigration and Refugee Board, October 1998, 57pp)

SUDAN

Since 26 November seven people have been ordered to report to security headquarters in Khartoum on a daily basis. They are **Rashad Hamed Alsayed**, an agricultural inspector, **Ali Khalifa**, a trade union activist, **Dr Nageeg Aldee**, a trade union activist, **Al Tayeb Abdalkafi**, a company director, **Hassan Shamat**, **Hassan Osman**, former employee of Sudan Airways and **Mohamed Osman Mahjoub**, a journalist. The seven are required to report to the security forces at 8am each day and remain there until 5 pm, without interogation

procedures. All have been detained on previous occasions. (OMCT)

Recent Publications: Zwier, Lawrence J, 1998 *North Against South (World in Conflict)* Lemer Publications; *Food and power in Sudan - A Critique of Humanitarianism* (African Rights, May 1997, 372pp)

SWAZILAND

On 21 October deputy chairperson of Swaziland's Constitution Review Commission Promise Msibi called for the restriction on South African journalists covering events in his country. The *Swazi Observer* newspaper quoted Msibi as calling on the government to take 'drastic steps' against South Africa Broadcasting Corporation (SABC) for 'insulting' the county's King Mswati III in their election coverage. He claimed that SABC reporter **Snuki Zikelala** had made remarks in his report that undermined the dignity and integrity of the king. (MISA)

SYRIA

There are increasing fears for the health of **Nizar Nayyouf**, (*Index* 6/1992, 8/1992, 10/1992, 10/1993, 6/1994, 6/1995, 5/1996, 3/1997), editor of *Voice of Democracy*, the newspaper of the Committee for the Defence of Democratic Freedoms and Human Rights (CDF), and a contributor to *Al-Hurriya* and *Al-Thaqafa Al-Ma'arifa*. Nayyouf was arrested on 10 January 1992 and sentenced by a military court on 17 March to 10 years' hard labour

for 'membership of an unauthorised organisation' and for 'disseminating false information'. He is suffering from Hodgkin's disease but the military authorities have denied him treatment until he pledges to refrain from political activity and to renounce his 'false statements' over the human rights situation. He has a six foot by nine foot cell and has not seen the sun for six years. Saber Filhout, president of the Syrian Journalists Union, was reported on 19 November as saying that no journalists or workers in the field have heard of the *Voice of Democracy*. (*Al-Quds al-ëArabi*)

TANZANIA

On October 7 Deputy Minister for Communication and Transport Maua Daftari threatened to take the *Guardian* newspaper to court for reporting that she swindled a friend of money. The minister demanded an apology on condition that 'it should be published on the same page and position as the contentious article' (MISA)

THAILAND

My Teacher Eats Biscuits, an independent film banned at the Bangkok Film Festival, will be viewed by the House Committee on Religion, Art and Culture to clarify whether it offends religious beliefs. Although the film was called in for censorship only a day before the Festival began, the censorship board denies banning the film officially. (*Nation*)

It was reported on 20

November that the film board has rejected two revised scripts for the new version of *The King and I,* leading 20th Century Fox to relocate the shooting of the film to Malaysia. Thailand still bans screening of the film of the same name, starring Yul Brynner and Deborah Kerr, on the grounds that King Mongkhut is depicted as a brutal tyrant rather than a scholar and linguist. Journalists are forbidden to insult royalty under the law of lèse majesté. *(Daily Telegraph)*

TOGO

Following the filing of a defamation complaint, **Appollinaire Mewenemesse**, editor-in-chief of bi-monthly *La Dépêche,* was arrested and taken to a police station in the capital Lomé on 21 October. The complaint was filed by the minster of defence after *La Dépêche* published an article on 15 October which attributed responsibility for robberies in the capital to the armed forces. Police seized all copies of the bi-monthly after the newspaper quoted a non-commissioned officer stating that 'fragments of abandoned arms found at the crime scene belonged either to the police or the army.' (RSF)

On 10 November journalist **Edoh Amewouho** was arrested and detained at the national police station. Amewouho, who writes for the private weekly Le *Nouveau Combat,* was moved the following day to Lóme prison. His arrest was in connection with the publication in the 6 to 13 August edition of two

articles which 'attacked the honour of the presidential couple'. On 6 August, **Augustine Asionbo**, editor of *Tingo Tingo*, **Pamphile Gnimassou**, editor of *Abito* and the *Le Nouveau Combat* journalist **Elias Hounkali** were arrested in connection with the publication of these articles (*Index* 6/1998). Two of those detained were released after a few days, but Hounkali is still being held without trial. (RSF)

TURKEY

Sabah newspaper published revelations on 15 October that Turkey had used technological capability to partially jam the transmissions of **Med-TV**, the Kurdish-language satellite station (*Index* 2/1997, 5/1997, 6/1998) The article reported that a senior official had said it was not possible to totally prevent the transmissions because of international conventions and satellite communications agreements. 'Turkey has the capability to entirely prevent these transmissions,' he said, 'but we would face strong reactions. Satellite wars would begin and Turksat satellites would be jammed in the same way.' *(Sabah)*

On 27 October **Akin Birdal**, president of the Human Rights Association, had his one-year jail sentence upheld by the Court of Appeals (*Index* 4/1998, 5/1998). On 9 November he was prevented from flying to Norway for essential medical treatment. (Observatory)

Deniz Ozcan, one of the main eye-witnesses in the trial

of the police officers accused of murdering journalist **Metin Goktepe** (*Index* 2/1996, 1/1997, 6/1997, 1/1998, 2/1998, 3/1998, 5/1998), was arrested by police in Istanbul on 1 November. Ozcan was forced into an unmarked car and told: 'You have said enough, now you are going to shut up'. He was taken to Yesidirek police station where he was slapped, kicked and beaten around the head with a walkie-talkie. He was eventually released later that night. (RSF)

Two journalists entering Turkey from northern Iraq were arrested and had their materials seized by soldiers on 6 November. **Nevzat Bingol** and **Veysi Ipek**, on assignment for ATV, were held and questioned at the Habur border posting by members of a special unit and the police information service. They were forced to spend the night on a bridge in the no-man's land that divides Turkey and Iraq. The same day four other journalists, **Esat Aydin** of ATV, **Ahmet Besenk** and **Adnan Sunsek** of the IHA press agency, and **Soner Gunes** of the CHA press agency, were arrested close to the border for having 'filmed without authorisation'. (RSF)

Several Turkish journalists and cameramen covering the events surrounding the arrest of Kurdish Workers' Party leader Abdullah Ocalan's in Rome were beaten by Kurdish demonstrators on 14 November. **Faruk Zabci** and **Fatih Altayli**, correspondents of the daily *Hurriyet*; reporters **Hayrettin Karateke** and

Metchan Demir; Abdurrahman Keskin of the official TRT station; Cengiz Ozkarabekir, cameraman for Interstar TV; Unsal Ergel and Ahn Ozyurt, both with NTV; were forced to take refuge in the Turkish embassy, (RSF)

Adnan Gerger and Fatih Cotur, reporter and cameraman for ATV television, Goksel Polat and Hakan Dikiciler, reporter and cameraman for Kanal D TV and Koran Karar, reporter for the daily *Sabah*, were arrested by police about 60 km outside Rome. The journalists were headed for the region were Abdullah Ocalan had been arrested. (RSF)

On 19 November Murat Bozlak, leader of the People's Democracy Party (HADEP), was arrested after the party had organised a nationwide hunger strike at their offices. Police arrested 60 people, including Ankara representative Kemal Bulbul, in raids in the capital - a further 190 were arrested during police searches in the towns of Bursa, Van and Antalya. The offices of Kurdish newspaper Ulkede *Gundem* were also searched. Editor Hayrettin Demircioglu, coordinating editor Yurdusev Ozsokmenler, editor Filiz Duman and reporters Yasemin Ozturk, Tulay Kilinc, Tulin Bozkurt, Kahraman Yapici and employees Ali Turgal, Sait Korkut and Serhat were all detained. In Batman Salih Erol, Narin Adsan and Filiz Yurek were held. In Mersin Ersin Ongel and Habip

Celik, in Urfa Seydo Basmanci and Azad, In Van Adil Harmanci, in Adana Bildane Dag and Nazim Deniz Surucu were all detained. The archives were ransacked and disks, photos, publications and diaries were confiscated. Countrywide more than 700 people were arrested in the crackdown after Italy refused to extradite Ocalan to Turkey. (Kurdistan Information Centre)

Police attacked the 180th protest of the 'Saturday Mothers' (Families of the Disappeared) on 28 November. The sit-down meeting has been banned during the previous 10 weeks, although the demonstrators still appear (*Index* 6/1998). (Med-TV)

On December 1 the trial of Professor Yalcin Kucuk, a prominent left-wing academic, opened in Ankara State Security Court. He is accused of disseminating separatist propaganda in a speech he made at a cultural festival in 1993. Kucuk returned from five years' self-imposed exile in France in October. (*Turkish Daily News*)

UGANDA

Ogen Kevin Aliro, chief sub-editor of the *Monitor*, an independent Kampala daily, sustained serious injuries on 29 October after he was attacked by unknown assailants. The attack is believed to be retaliation for Aliro's investigative report titled 'Safe Houses: A Return to the Shadows', published in the 27 October edition, which reported that the practice of

torture was re-emerging at 'ungazetted safe houses' run by the internal security organisation and the department of military intelligence. (CPJ, *Independent*)

New Zealand journalist Paul Henry is reported to have flown into Uganda in early November to offer Rwandan rebels, aligned to Interahamwe, air time on Radio Pacific Network in return for the release of three kidnapped tourists. (IRIN, *New Vision*)

UNITED KINGDOM

A 141-year-old photograph of the engineer Isambard Kingdom Brunel has been censored by a museum's management, it was reported on 9 October. The 1857 portrait shows Brunel at Bristol Docks in familiar attire and with his trademark cigar in his mouth. The management of the Maritime Heritage Centre decided that cigar-smoking was not a suitable image to present to its young visitors and so Brunel's cigar was airbrushed out. (*Guardian, Telegraph*)

On 20 October the notable libel lawyer Peter Carter-Ruck called for the introduction of a statutory defence for newspapers which publish public interest stories that later prove to be untrue. Speaking at the London Press Club, he said that as long as newspapers could prove that the story was written 'in good faith, without malice and based on evidence which might reasonably be believed to be true'. then they should be able to use that as defence against against prosecution for libel. (*Guardian*)

On 27 October a court ruled that Channel Four's *Trial and Error* had not libelled a former police officer. The programme had alleged that former inspector Trevor Gladding had perjured himself and conspired to pervert the course of justice in the case of Gary Mills and Tony Poole, later convicted of murder. The Police Federation now faces a legal bill of £1.2m after the case which **David Jessel**, the programme's maker, described as a 'victory for investigative journalism'. (*Guardian*)

On 11-12 November various journals reported the machinations within the Labour Party over the election of a new London mayor. Ken Livingstone, the former leader of the Greater London Council, is the frontrunner for the post but the new Labour establishment moved quickly to establish a method of candidate selection that guarantees that he will not be chosen. Moves by the party to isolate Livingstone follow similar actions to prevent the Welsh MP Rhodri Morgan from becoming leader of the new Welsh assembly and the barring of current MP Dennis Canavan from standing for the new Scottish parliament. All are outspoken critics of new Labour and the party's actions have laid its leaders open to charges of being 'control freaks'. (*The Times, Guardian, Daily Telegraph, Financial Times*)

On 24 November the Commission for Racial Equality ruled that a school was wrong to invite a member of the racist British National Party to address its pupils. Dulwich College in South London had invited the BNP's press officer to speak to pupils in what a spokesperson for the school said was part of a 'series of meetings exploring political extremes'. (*Daily Telegraph*)

On 25 November it was reported that the Labour Party's Internet website had been 'purged' of a pre-election policy document, Communicating Britain's Future, which detailed Labour's support for encryption technology, and their opposition to restrictions on the use and export of strong encryption which the document calls 'wrong in principle' and 'unworkable in practice'. The document was removed following the inclusion in the Queen's Speech of the Electronic Commerce Bill which proposes the control of encryption, and registration of digital signature systems. The move has outraged academics, privacy campaigners and the computer industry. (*Daily Telegraph*)

In an historic decision on 25 November, the House of Lords ruled by a three to two majority that the former Chilean dictator, General Augusto Pinochet, was not immune from extradition to Spain where he is wanted in connection with the torture and murder of Spanish nationals. The Law Lords' decision overturns the decision by the High Court on 28 October that Pinochet was immune from extradition under the terms of the 1978

State Immunity Act which gives immunity for leaders carrying out actions recognised as legitimate functions. Lord Nicholls, ruling against Pinochet, said that 'it hardly needs saying that torture of his own subjects, or of aliens, would not be regarded by international law as a function of a head of state'. (*Financial Times, International Herald Tribune, Guardian*)

The BBC was embroiled in a row after the *Newsnight* programme on the 27 October. In an interview with presenter Jeremy Paxman, the newspaper columnist and former MP Matthew Parris stated that the Trade and Industry secretary Peter Mandelson was 'certainly gay'. The resultant furore led the BBC's political adviser Anne Sloman to issue a memo that said 'under no circumstances ... should the allegations about the private life of Peter Mandelson be repeated, or referred to, on any broadcast'. The memo provoked anger in many quarters, notably from the respected broadcaster Jonathan Dimbleby, presenter of Radio 4's *Any Questions*, who said that implementation of the memo 'would require censorship of matters that are of legitimate public interest'. Parris, a columnist for the *Sun* newspaper, was sacked by the paper which was reported to have changed its policy on 'outing' gay politicians. (*Guardian, Daily Telegraph*)

USA

Hollywood is tightening its restrictive grip on video licensing by demanding that,

MUMIA ABU-JAMAL

The war on the poor

In every phase and facet of national life, there is a war being waged on America's poor. Poor mothers are targeted for criminal sanctions for acts, which, if committed by mothers of higher economic class, would merit treatment at the Betty Ford Centre. In youth policy, governments hasten to close schools while building prisons as their 'graduate schools'. Xenophobic politicians hoist campaigns to the dark star of imprisonment for street beggars, further fattening the fortress economy. The only apparent solution to the scourge of homelessness is to build more and more prisons.

In America's 90's, to be poor is not so much a socio-economic status as it is a serious character flaw. Statistics tell a tale of loss and want so dreadful, that Dickens, of *A Tale of Two Cities* fame, would cringe. Consider: seven million people homeless with less than two hundred dollars in monthly income. Thirty seven million people – 14.5 per cent of the nation's population – living below poverty levels. Of those, 29 per cent are African Americans, meaning over 10.6 million blacks living in poverty. Both wings of the ruling 'Republicrat' Party try to outdo themselves with ever more draconian measures to restrict, repress, restrain and eliminate the poor.

Outgunned in the industrial wars by Japan and Germany, the US has embarked on a low technology, low skilled, high employment scheme that exploits the poor, the stupid and the slow via a boom in prison construction. More and more Americans are guarding more and more American prisoners for more and more years. And this in the midst of the lowest crime rate in decades.

The time is ripe for a new, brighter, life-affirming vision that liberates not represses, the poor who, after all, are the vast majority of this Earth's people. Neither serpentine politics, nor sterile economic theory which treats them – people – as mere economic units, offer much hope. For the very politicians they vote for spit in their faces while economists write them off as 'non-persons'. ❏

Mumia Abu-Jamal's latest appeal against the death sentence was denied by the Pennsylvania Supreme Court on 30 October. A case for a re-trial will now go to the federal judicial system. Taken from the album 'All things censored' Alternative Tentacles/Prison radio from the end of 1999, all Digital Video Disc drives (DVD-ROM) in computers be regionally coded. The film industry employs six codes around the world to control the release dates of films in different countries. At the moment a DVD-ROM drive, bought with a PC, has a software switch which allows the owner to reset the code up to five times, before locking on the fifth setting. (*New Scientist*)

A Virginia District Court judge has ruled that libraries cannot use crude filters to block connection to Internet sites they think are harmful to children. In the case brought by the American Civil Liberties Union for eight organisations who thought their sites had been unfairly blocked, the judge found that the Loudon County Library was violating the constitutional rights of adult patrons to view what they wanted. Some affected sites advocated safe sex, represented women's groups or reviewed gay and lesbian books for teens. (*New Scientist*)

On 17 November a federal judge ordered Microsoft to change its Windows operating system within 90 days, or take it off the market. The court order was in response to a lawsuit filed by Sun Microsystems in October 1997. Sun claimed the terms of the licence agreement to its Java software were broken when Microsoft modified Java to maximise its power in Windows programmes. (*Financial Times*)

UZBEKISTAN

A 60-year-old academic may be extradited from Russia to stand trial on charges of attempting to overturn the constitutional order, *Nezavisimaya Gazeta* reported on 14 November. If convicted, **Aliboy Yulyakhshiev** could face a prison sentence of five to 10 years. Tashkent issued an arrest warrant for Yulyakhshiev in 1995 for his involvement in the shipment of the opposition newspaper *Erk* to Uzbekistan from a printing house in Kyiv, Ukraine. (RFE/RL)

VIETNAM

At a meeting with senior editors of the official Vietnam News Agency in Hanoi on 27 November, Communist Party chief Le Kha Phieu warned journalists to toe the party line and avoid dwelling on sensational and negative reporting. He was quoted as saying that a true journalist needed to be on 'the right political track oriented by the party'. (Reuters)

A recent International Press Institute report noted that whilst the press is generally freer nowadays, journalists are still hindered by laws such as one whereby journalists can be charged with treason if they reveal 'sensitive information'. Consequently, most journalists practise a conservative self-censorship which does not challenge the government's tight grip over the media. (IPI)

ZIMBABWE

Minister of Information, Posts and Communication Shen Shimutengwende has instructed the entire board of the Zimbabwe Broadcasting Corporation (ZBC) to resign. The *Herald* newspaper quoted the minister as saying this will be the first step to 'restructuring' ZBC along commercial lines and gave the board a 15 November deadline to leave. Press reports however say the board members have rejected the order to resign. The *Financial Gazette* reported on 15 October that, although the ZBC Act gives the minister powers to fire the board, the reasons he advanced for his actions were not valid. The paper quotes unnamed sources that the reason for prematurely terminating the board's term are mainly personal clashes between its members and the minister. (MISA)

Compiled by: John Kamau, Regina Jere-Malanda, Daniel Rogers (Africa); Rupert Clayton, Andrew Kendle, Ruth Pilch, Catherine Richards (Asia); Simon Martin (eastern Europe and CIS); Dolores Cortés (south and central America); Arif Azad, Gill Newsham, Neil Sammonds (Middle East); Andrew Elkin (north America and Pacific); Tony Callaghan (UK and western Europe).

Brazil: Facing up to race

Brazil, the world's eleventh largest economy, has produced levels of racial inequality comparable to South Africa under apartheid. The national myth of 'racial democracy' is now being openly challenged by Brazil's 'other half' who are poor, excluded – and angry

File compiled by Michael Griffin

Sleeping rough, Rocinha, Rio – Credit: Panos

GILBERTO GIL & CAETANO VELOSO

Haiti

When you're invited up into the Jorge Amado Centre
To watch from above the line of soldiers, nearly all of them
black
Beating black layabouts across the back of the head
Mulatto thieves and others who are nearly white
But treated like blacks
Just to show the other nearly blacks
(And they're nearly all blacks)
And the nearly whites who're poor as blacks
How blacks, poor and mulattos
And nearly whites nearly blacks they're so poor, how they're
treated
And it don't matter if the eyes of the whole world
Are turned for a moment towards the square
Where the slaves were punished
And where today there's a drumming a drumming
With the purity of schoolkids dressed for parade-day
And the epic grandeur of a people growing, taking shape
Attracts us, dazzles and excites us
Nothing matters: not the profile of that mansion
Nor the lens of the fantastic, nor Paul Simon's album
No-one, No-one's a citizen
If you go and see the party in the Pelourinho, and if you don't
go
Think of Haiti, pray for Haiti
Haiti is here - Haiti's not here

And if you see a congressman on TV in barely disguised panic
Faced with any, but I mean any, any, any
Easy-looking education plan

Easy and quick-looking
And that's going to mean a threat of democratisation
Of primary-school education
And if that same congressman defends the adoption of capital
punishment
And the reverend cardinal says he can see all that spirit in the
foetus
And none in the criminal
And if, as you jump the light, that same old red light,
You notice a man pissing at the street corner on a gleaming
sack of Leblon's rubbish
And when you hear São Paulo's smiling silence
In the face of the massacre
Of 111 defenceless prisoners, but nearly all black prisoners
Or nearly black, or nearly white nearly black they're so poor
And the poor are like rubbish and everyone knows how you
treat blacks
And when you're going to take a tour around the Caribbean
And you're about to screw without a condom
And offer your clever contribution to the blockade against
Cuba
Think of Haiti, pray for Haiti
Haiti is here, Haiti's not here ❏

From the album Tropicália 2, *1993*
Translated by David Treece

DANIELA CESTAROLLO

The right colour

Five hundred years after the arrival of the Portuguese, Brazilians are only just beginning to address the legacy of slavery

Brazil is at last revealing its other face. After 500 years of seeking to shape itself in the image of a white, western Catholic country, Brazil is having to come to terms with its immense ethnic diversity and the social and economic implications this brings with it. An extensive report published in 1996 by the daily *Folha de São Paulo* revealed to the nation that almost half its 160 million people are black. This amounts to the realisation that Brazil had the largest black population in the world after Nigeria. The report also presented figures on racial prejudice, illiteracy, unemployment and income distribution among blacks from all over Brazil. The figures shocked a nation that has always believed itself to be the racial democracy of the southern hemisphere.

The myth of racial democracy has since the 1930s marketed Brazil as the sunny country where people of all races mix happily together on the beach, on the football pitch and in the Carnival parade. However, the myth has in reality served as a buttress for one of the most perverse and sophisticated forms of modern racism. By contrast to the apartheid system of South Africa, Brazil reveals a number of examples of disguised discrimination, such as in job advertising or television programming. Job adverts, which often ask for a 'good appearance', in reality mean that blacks are not expected to apply. Television dramas, meanwhile, typically portray blacks within extremely limited, stereotyped roles, such as domestic servants or thieves. Not surprisingly, a recent poll on racial origins showed that only 5 per cent of Brazilians identified themselves as black. Most preferred to be called brown, bronze or coffee-coloured.

Discrimination based on skin colour was made a criminal offence in 1951, but the law was completely ignored and almost no-one was aware of its existence. During the military dictatorship (1964–1985), any discussion about racial confrontation was considered subversive by the ruling establishment. The constitution of 1988 upgraded the criminal status of racial discrimination but very few cases actually have gone to court since then. The National Human Rights Programme promoted by the present government since January 1995 has taken a liberal and more democratic approach. It determined that mixed-race, or *mestiço*, people should be considered by the Institute of Geography and Statistics, which is responsible for the demographic census, as part of the black population. This was the first time that a Brazilian government had officially acknowledged the reality of a national identity ethnically founded on Afro-Brazilian roots.

In the wake of the report the press inundated the country with new statistics and interviews with prominent and successful figures from the black community. One was the former football player Pelé, who was appointed Minister of Sport by Fernando Henrique Cardoso during his first term of office. Despite being a national and international celebrity Pelé has never used his influence to further greater racial equality. In a country where racial discrimination goes hand in hand with social exclusion, Pelé has opted for 'social whitening', marrying and socialising mainly within white circles.

For the wider majority, meanwhile, racial discrimination clearly operates in conjunction with other socio-economic factors such as income distribution and gender. Afro-Brazilian women come off worst, earning half the wages received by white women employees in the same job, and one third of the white male wage-rate. Such blatantly discriminatory wage differentials are just one of the persistent legacies of Brazil's colonial past. As one of the largest importers of slaves in the Americas, it received perhaps as many as 10 million slaves from West Africa and Angola. It was also the last country in South America to abolish slavery, in 1888. Little more than a century on, the most visited symbol of that era is the so-called *pelourinho*, in the centre of the northeastern city of Salvador; once the public whipping-post for black slaves, it now buzzes with tourists and night life. The surrounding area has become one of Brazil's principal heritage sites, a reminder, perhaps, of a history many would prefer to forget.

Yet, as elsewhere, that history of persecution and discrimination has spawned resistance. Dance, music and religion rooted in African traditions have helped black Brazilians to withstand the homogenising impact of a western mass culture that has often been a vehicle for ideas inimical to the principle of ethnic diversity and has encouraged an ignorance of the country's non-white traditions. In 1995, *Raça,* the first-ever magazine intended for a black audience, was launched. The new publication is a hybrid of adolescent and women's lifestyle magazines, with beauty tips, fashion features and political debates on the role of blacks in contemporary society. Although a timid venture by comparison with similar publications in the USA or UK, it is nevertheless a great step forward – at least for those who can afford to buy and read it. Illiteracy among blacks is as high as 30 per cent, nearly double the national average of 17 per cent. As one black activist in Salvador proudly shouted: '*Raça* makes young people proud to be Black!'

Whilst the launch of *Raça* represents a commercial venture aimed at identifying a black 'community' in terms of the consumer market, at a grassroots level since the 1980s there has been an upsurge of autonomous initiatives that are voicing black concerns and demands in a more militantly politicised manner. Among this new generation of black campaigning organisations is the Geledes Black Women's Institute. Cultural self-expression, which has historically played such a central role in building resistance and reshaping the identity of Brazil's slave and ex-slave population, has once again returned to the fore. The explosion of hip-hop culture, which only recently reached the mainstream commercial market in Brazil, has opened up a rich and vibrant channel for young blacks to speak of racism, police violence, gang warfare and drugs trafficking, often in the context of political activity and community projects.

Some estimates put the number of rap groups in Greater São Paulo at 30,000, many of them linked to 'possess', '*gangues*' or cultural associations which, in their turn, may have loose connections with political organisations and parties. The Negroatividades Cultural Association from Centreville, Santo André, for example, was founded by rapper Marcelinho of the '*Profetas da Revoluçao*', and Marcel, a member of the Union of Socialist Youth (an offshoot of the Maoist Communist Party of Brazil), in the wake of a show promoted by Workers' Party Mayor Luíza Erundina to commemorate the anniversary of São Paulo on 25 January 1989. The *Movimento Hip Hop Organizado* (MH20), which emerged out of this initiative, began to mobilise black kids around community-based projects combining artistic self-improvement with social provision.

While the movement in defence of black rights and interests has an important international as well as local dimension, the case of Brazil's Indians and Indian descendants has a different kind of complexity, as the assaults on their rights directly involve the source of their traditional livelihood and cultural identity – the land. If being black and poor makes one a target for abusive policing methods, the status of Indian is more akin to that of a primitive animal in the bush, an obstacle to progress, lazy, backward and undesirable, fit only to be eliminated. When the Portuguese reached the South American coast in the sixteenth century, there were over 5 million Indians in what later became the Portuguese colony. They belonged to over a 1,000 different nations, each with its own language and culture, and made their living from subsistence agriculture, hunting, fishing and gathering. Five hundred years later, there are only 200 indigenous nations left and a population of 300,000, of whom 30 per cent suffer from severe malnutrition and hunger. The genocide of the indigenous people, in Brazil and the rest of the world, is probably one of the most horrific crimes of our times.

Contact with non-Indian society during the first four centuries drastically reduced the indigenous population through the impact of disease and military conflict. In the twentieth century, however, it has been the invasion of indigenous lands by state development projects, gold miners, cattle ranchers and logging companies that has most threatened the survival of the first inhabitants. Whereas the western mentality has viewed the land chiefly as a commodity, for the indigenous peoples their relationship with the land is both material and spiritual; it is at one and the same time the basis of their economy and their ancestral home. The precondition for any debate about the defence of indigenous identity must, therefore, be the basic right to the preservation and exclusive ownership of their territories and livelihoods.

Brazil's 1988 constitution states clearly in Article 231, Chapter VII: 'Recognition is given to the Indians' social organisation, customs, languages, beliefs and to their original rights over the lands they traditionally occupy, it being the duty of the Union [the Brazilian State] to demarcate them, and to protect and ensure that their wealth is respected.' In the light of the above, the chapter on Indian rights from the 1996 National Human Rights Programme sounds rather redundant. It emphasises once more the right to the land indigenous people occupy, a right already guaranteed by the Federal Constitution. In contrast to the paternalistic policies of the past, it also states that short-term actions for indigenous peoples in Brazil should support the reform of the Indian Statute and the implementation and promotion of Indian rights, as well as guaranteeing education and health care and the elimination of violence and discrimination against the Indians.

The National Indian Foundation, FUNAI, is the state agency responsible for the welfare of the Indians. However, its paternalistic approach has only contributed to the impoverishment and misery of the indigenous population of Brazil. The same FUNAI which is meant to supply health, education and legal assistance often neglects its role and aggravates the situation of dependence in which many communities now live in remote parts of the country. Between 1997 and 1998, the same government that promoted the publication of its human rights document approved a radical cut of over 80 per cent in spending on legal procedures involving the demarcation of indigenous lands in Brazil.

The state's omission in the demarcation of Indian lands and in the formulation of clear public policies in support of education, health care and economic development fosters a climate of constant violence against the indigenous populations. The picture is a precarious one: approximately 50 per cent of Indian areas have yet to be demarcated. At this end of the millennium, after all the ravages of colonial history, the spectre of genocide still haunts the first inhabitants of the territory called Brazil. ❑

Daniela Cestarollo *is a geographer and communications officer for Brazil at Christian Aid. A longer version of this article was published in* Long Night of Waiting *(Brazil Network, 1a Waterlow Rd, London N19 5NJ)*

FRANCISCO OLIVEIRA

A Bible and an automatic

Ignored by the system and hounded by the police, blacks are organising through music to end the 'invisibility' imposed on them

A cultural revolution is emerging from the impoverished *favelas*. 'Around 60 per cent of young blacks, with no criminal records, have suffered some kind of police brutality ... Every four hours, a young black is killed in São Paulo.' These words are intoned by rapper Primo Preto on the third track of *Sobrevivendo no Inferno* (Surviving in Hell), by the rap group Racionais MC'S.

'God made the sea, the trees, children and love. Man gave us the slums, crack, treachery, guns, booze, whores. Me? I got an old Bible, an automatic and some bad feelings. And I'm trying to survive in hell.' That's the beginning of *Sobrevivendo no Inferno*. The CD sold 500,000 copies by word of mouth alone, more than any other rap record on a commercial label, and the only reason I can reproduce the song in its entirety is that it lasts just 23 seconds. Other lyrics, like *Tô Ouvindo Alguém Me Chamar* (I Can Hear Someone Call Me) or *Fórmula Mágica da Paz* (Magic Formula For Peace), just wouldn't be suitable.

More than a warning, the CD is a scream against the way blacks are treated by the system. Policemen consider blacks as prime suspects in any crime and the popularity they enjoy can be guaged in the polemical chorus of *Homens Fardados* (Men in Uniform), by the Pernambuco rap group, Faces do Subúrbio: 'Men in uniforms, they insist on doing justice with their own hands, are always the hot shots, the ones who're always right.'

The black is relegated to poverty and violence of the poor neighborhoods. But 'if you're handed a lemon,' as the saying goes, 'make lemonade'. It is from the poorest neighbourhoods that the cultural revolution is emerging and it's possibley thanks to the strength that comes from the oppressed. Inspired by Racionais MC'S and Faces do Subúrbio, other hip-hop groups are now betting high on independence and they don't give a damn about big labels.

Who are these rappers who refuse to flirt with the media, shun million-dollar contracts and survive by recording for independent labels? Racionais MC'S, made up of Mano Brown, Ice Blue, Edy Rock and Kl Jay, started in the shantytowns around São Paulo and their lyrics are successful because they describe what goes on in daily life. They're faithful to their origins, both in the language they use and their refusal to succumb to the big labels or TV networks.

Racionais appeared last year on MTV and the Video Music Brasil, where the clip *Diário de Um Detento* (A Prisoner's Diary) won two prizes. The awards made mainstream labels even more anxious to sign them as their golden boys. Mano Brown summed it up: 'Their money doesn't seduce me. I'm not an idol, I'm a point of reference. I can rhyme 'cause I rhyme according to life in the slums, stuff from the streets. Get it?' Xis, of the rap group DMN, says that Racionais 'are as important to Brazilian rap as the Public Enemy was to American.'

The São Paulo group Thaide & DJ Hum is also independent and has its own label, Brava Gente. Pioneers of rap, the vigorous scratches made by DJ Hum meld perfectly with the quick, intelligent verse written by Thaide. The duo has never been asked to participate in mainstream TV shows, but the CD *Preste Atenção* (Pay Attention) has sold over 80,000 copies, again on a word-of-mouth basis. In Brasília, the independent label Discovery is marketing groups such as Álibi, Cirurgia Moral and Baseado Nas Ruas, distributing over 50,000 copies. There's also the label Só Balanço, founded by the rapper Gog, who became unhappy with Discovery. Gog believes rap isn't only music, but also part of a social movement, and that has to be understood by the public in general.

If there's total aversion by the media in general towards the new wave of Brazilian rap, who plays the songs or promotes the hip-hop bands? Hidden amid the 'huts' of the shantytowns, community radio stations like Radio Favela, now transmitting to 160,000 listeners in the city of Belo Horizonte, have become the alternative 'voice of the slums'. They offer a service to Brazil's disaffected, both in language and content, while their programming airs the problems that most affect the *favelas* – drugs, violence, racial discrimination, health and the lack of other services.

They're the ones who promote and help groups that appeal to the community, and they then pass the word on to other ghetto stations. Groups like DMN, RZO, and Comando DMC gained popularity exclusively through community radios – and the ensuing word of mouth. RZO, from São Paulo, followed their initial launch on community radio by paying themselves for the pressing of 5,000 vinyl records themselves. What happened? They became famous three years ago with the hit *O Trem* (The Train).

The boys that belong to hip-hop are making a point of being independent not only to avoid the media, but to strengthen the black movement. The more independent labels there are, the more quality bands are likely to record in the future. Sampa Crew, which has already recorded for the all-powerful Sony, is today with Big Posse records. Kudos to Sampa, who are already influencing and sponsoring new groups.

Meanwhile, the media still chase Mano Brown and his troupe, who say they couldn't care less. When asked if the award-winning *Diário de Um Detento* could be shown in the popular TV show Fantástico, a laconic Brown answered: 'If they wanna run it, OK. We're not showing up, dig?' ❏

Francisco Oliveira is editor of Brazil's first black consciousness magazine, Raça. *Translated by Katia Stegun*

JAN ROCHA

One day in the life of Wagner

For millions of shantytown dwellers, the police represent the only contact they have with the state. And it's often a lethal contact

On 27 August 1997, in a little two-room house at the top of the Santa Marta shantytown in Rio, Wagner Marcos da Silva gulped down a *cafezinho*, cast a fond look at his surfboard propped in the corner, kissed his mother and set out for work. At the top of the hill, above the *favela*, stood the giant statue of Christ, arms outstretched as though in protection. Far below the waves crashed on to the beach at Arpoador, Wagner's favourite surfing spot.

Late for work, he bounded down the steep concrete steps between the cramped shacks, tossing greetings to the women in their homes, the old men labouring up the steps. Everyone knew Wagner. He and his sister Valeria had grown up here. His mother, Ana had generations of children in her tiny home. Halfway down he bumped into his friend Renato, returning from the baker's with fresh bread. In high spirits, Wagner playfully kicked Renato and then, to escape retaliation, ran across the tiny landing and down the next flight of steps.

That was the moment his life changed for ever. A four-man police patrol, hunting for drug dealers, was silently working its way up. For them, the possibility that Wagner could be a law-abiding, honest citizen on his way to work was completely outweighed by three other characteristics: he lived in a shantytown, he was young and he was black. And he was running towards them.

So they shot him. Twice. They must have realised their mistake very quickly from the horrified reaction of those who saw it happen. But their first concern was not to rush him to hospital but to fabricate evidence to turn Wagner into a drug dealer. People were ordered into their houses and forbidden to look out of their windows. Then, while Wagner lay bleeding, a policeman fired a .38 revolver into a ditch twice and placed it in his hand. A bag containing drugs, apparently jettisoned by the real drug dealer who fled as the police approached, was placed next to his body. One witness, an 11-year-old boy peeping through a hole in his window, said he saw a policeman smash Wagner's teeth with a gun. Only then did the police ask for a sheet in which to place the injured man and carry him down the steps to the street. And, the witnesses say, they held his feet, but allowed his head to bang down the 60 concrete steps.

No ambulance was called: Wagner's bloodsoaked body was stuffed into the boot of a car and driven to the Miguel Couto hospital. Everyone, including the police was sure he would die. The hospital was used to receiving bullet-ridden bodies brought in by the police. The hospital director said that 99 per cent of them are dead or die soon after. But Wagner, strong from surfing, held on to life.

A police commander boasted, 'This boy is still alive only because we rescued him. If the police wanted to kill him, they would have done it. A dead man can't talk.' Semi-paralysed, teeth broken, brain-damaged, Wagner refused to die. So he was charged with attempted homicide and drug dealing: now a criminal suspect he was handcuffed to the hospital bed and kept under armed guard. Later he was transferred to a prison hospital: repeated requests to allow him bail to get proper medical treatment were refused by the judge until November 1998, 15 months after he had been shot.

Nilo Batista, a well-known criminal lawyer and former governor of Rio, was so convinced of Wagner's innocence that he took up his case. But he is also convinced that the only abnormal aspect of it is that Wagner lived. He says it is normal for police to fabricate evidence: almost all their victims die, and there is no investigation because the police always fired in 'legitimate self-defence'. These deaths merit a paragraph or two in the press when it is reported that two, or four or five drug dealers died during a gun battle with the police in such and such a shantytown. Many of them are probably Wagners, guilty only of being young, black and living in the *favela*.

For the Rio police there was, until recently, an actual incentive to kill. To kill a suspect during a 'gunbattle' was considered an act of bravery, rewarded with pay rises and promotion. This meant that, while the overall figure for homicide in Rio has gone down, the number of police victims has risen since the reward was introduced. An independent research centre found that the police killed more than 1,100 people in Rio in just over 3 years – and that almost none of them had a criminal record.

Because Wagner lived, and his case was taken up by a well known lawyer, his fate attracted media attention. Most other police victims remain anonymous. In Brazil, demands for justice usually depend not on who carried out the violence, but who the victim is. Nancy Cardia, a social pyschologist working at NEV, a centre for violence studies in São Paulo, has concluded that certain groups are simply considered to be outside the 'moral community'. This means that they can be 'ill-treated, humiliated, tortured or killed without the feeling that this violates consensual rules of justice'. *Favelados*, or shantytown dwellers, constitute one such group. Prisoners are another.

When the military police were called to quell a riot at São Paulo's Carandiru prison in October 1992, they decided to teach them a lesson. They killed 111 unarmed prisoners, many of them shot as they cowered in their cells pleading for their lives. Opinion polls showed that a majority of the population approved. Prisoners in São Paulo's police cells are held in such appallingly over-crowded conditions – 100 or 200 men crammed into cells designed for 30 or 40 – they have to take it in turns to sleep. Although many have TB and other infectious diseases, medical attention is almost non-existent.

Bloody and brutal riots and break-out attempts happen almost every day. But administrators are reluctant to spend money on prisons because 'being soft on bandits' does not bring votes. The vast majority of prisoners are poor. Very few middle class people are sent to prison and, under a special law, anyone with a university degree is entitled to a special cell, so they never have to mix with the others. Torture is still commonly used by the police to extract information and confessions. Although this fact is widely known, nothing is done about it; nor does it cause indignation.

For Nancy Cardia this injustice is legitimised by a deeply held belief in certain social myths, which are duly encouraged by those who are interested in maintaining exclusion. These myths include social and racial inferiority and the 'threat' posed by certain groups who are considered 'subhuman' or 'animals'. Human rights for these 'others' is dismissed as 'human rights for bandits', a favourite catchphrase of those who denigrate the work of human rights activists.

In this context the law is not for everyone. Instead, inequality before the law is guaranteed by Brazil's basic economic, social and political inequalities. And violence has a crucial role to play in the process of making ample sectors of the population feel powerless before the authorities. The role of the military police is much more about control of the mob than defending citizens. The result is a restricted, fragile citizenship for whom lack of action in the face of injustice is the norm, and not the exception. This passivity, this lack of indignation make building a truly democratic society much more difficult. After all, the precondition for such a society must be not only a consensus about what is right and what is wrong, but also a shared sense of compassion.

In the *favelas* people are trapped between the violence of the drug gangs and the violence of the police. For Brazil's millions of shantytown and slum dwellers, the police all too often represent the only contact they have with the state. A positive presence in the form of schools, health, social services, even public utilities and rubbish collection, is rare. In the absence of the authorities, drug gangs take control. They see the *favelados'* attempts to organise as a threat. Many community leaders have been murdered for trying to remain independent of the drug gangs.

But in Santa Marta, Wagner's shantytown, indignation was stronger than fear of the police or of the drug bosses. Over 500 people signed a petition saying they knew him to be an honest worker, not a drug dealer. And eight people gave evidence to the court, describing Wagner's Calvary. On December 2nd, a judge ordered Wagner's provisional release to await trial, which is expected some time in March 1999. ❑

Jan Rocha was the Guardian's *Brazil correspondent from 1984 to 1994 and, in recent years, has worked as researcher and assistant producer on numerous TV documentaries*

'Brazil is absorbing the Negro race; there is no colour bar to advancement, there is no social bar to advancement" – Theodore Roosevelt, 1913

<u>Slavery abolished</u> 1888

<u>Population</u> 161.7 million of which 44 per cent black (gov't census) or 70 per cent (UNESCO). The census has 5 categories of skin colour; Brazilian's themselves have over 135 different ways of describing their skin.

<u>Literacy</u> White Brazilians 85 per cent, black Brazilians 63 per cent; 70 per cent of non-white 8-year-olds fall one year behind their peers

<u>Life expectancy</u> is 8 years shorter for blacks

<u>Health</u> In São Paulo, 40 per cent of the health budget is spent on 3 per cent of the population for complex treatments like organ transplants

<u>Infant mortality</u>: 36 per thousand infants; 38 per cent of all deaths

<u>Women</u> Two per cent of black women have professional jobs; 80 per cent of domestic work is done by black people; 23 per cent of women in industry with college degrees are white, 1 per cent black

<u>Wages/Income</u> In 1988, average income for white males was twice that of black males; 24.6 per cent of whites earn below minimum wage, 44.8 per cent of blacks. On average, a black male wage is 40 per cent of a white male wage; a black female wage is 25 per cent of a white man's earnings.

Sixty million Brazilians live below the poverty line

75 per cent of voters earn less than US$3000 per year

48 per cent of National Domestic Income (NDI) is earned by the richest 10 per cent; the poorest 20 per cent earn 2.6 per cent; 80 per cent of income is controlled by the richest 1 per cent of the population

Government One cabinet minister of mixed descent; seven of 559 National Congress members identify as black; no black state governors

Work 18 per cent of business men/senior administrators are non-white
200 out of 14,000 priests are black; 5 out of 400 Catholic bishops are black

Racial Prejudice 89 per cent of self-identified whites admit prejudice exists; only 11 per cent of whites admit they are themselves prejudiced

Farmland Of 330 million hectares, almost 50 per cent is unused; over 2 million rural families are landless

Sources: Instituto Brasileiro de Geografia e Estatistica;*Benedita de Silva* (1997); *The Brazil Reader: History, Culture, Politics*; *Death Without Weeping;The Violence of Everyday Life in Brazil*; *EIU Country Profile: Brazil 1998-99;Reassessing Brazil: New Risks and Opportunities*; IMF Staff Country Report No.98/24; *Brazil: Recent Economic Developments; Race in Contemporary Brazil: From Indifference to Inequality*. With thanks to the Latin America Bureau. Researched by **Ipsita Mondal**

Photo credit: Panos/Sean Sprague

PMC, DJ DECO MURPHY, X, VISAO DE RUA AND MV BILL

All this here is ours too

I'm gonna tell another part of the story, I don't know if it'll make you laugh or weep
But I know that the account that follows could only be told by someone who's felt on his skin
The deep pain, the pain it's impossible to escape, put there in a way
That's strategically prepared, cautiously calculated, coldly executed.
That's why we kept there for a long time, silent and imprisoned by the limits of our thoughts
If it were down to some all this would never change, for them it makes no odds,
But we're the ones who know what we're about, we've gotta make them hear our voice
You don't earn respect you win it, the time is now you'd better believe it
It was a hard road to get here but now we can say that this is our place
If you find out how we got here, you'll understand me better when you hear me say
That everything I've a right to, I want to have and can, because all this here is ours too
Everything I've a right to, I want to have and can - all this here is ours too.

In Brazil being black and poor is really hard, whoever's black and poor here suffers twice over,
In the hands of those guys he's always beaten down,
Black for them means to take what's coming, be called a monkey, be treated like a slave
The bossman's always around, dreadlocks or cropped hair is no good to him

The black who's proud is threatening too, the nice guy's gotta be ashamed of his colour
So I ask you, what's gonna happen now if we don't change, don't fight, if we knuckle under
The solution's inside of us, don't feel inferior next to any playboy
Turn on to what's around you, our space is getting bigger, changing for the better
Everything I've a right to, I want to have and can - all this here is ours too.

Everything I've a right to, I want to have and can - all this here is ours too ❏

Different worlds in Sã Paulo –
Credit: Julio Etchart/Pano

Isso aqui tambèm è nosso, *by* **P.MC & Dj Deco Murphy** *from their album* Identidade, *was translated by* **David Treece**.

LEONARDO BOFF

Global challenge

Far from spelling the end of revolutionary Catholicism, the triumph of international capital has laid the basis for a qualitative leap forward in the evolution of the spirit

Liberation Theology is the dominant theology in Brazil both among catholics and within the ecumenical sphere of the historical church. It no longer makes the headlines as in the 1970s and 1980s, when it was a public debate in the streets, but it has not lost its vitality. That is not due to the theology, but the pastoral practice of the Church.

Liberation Theology is a theory that articulates the liberating practice of the church, expressed in a preferential option for the poor, both in the fight against poverty and in favour of their freedom. Its pastoral activities are a mark of the seriousness of the church's historical commitment: to the landless, the homeless, native Indians, the blacks, marginalised women and street children. Pastoral work aims at setting up a health service in more than 100,000 base communities and some two million Bible groups.

As long as Christians commit themselves, in the name of the Gospel, to the struggle for liberation, as long as Christians reflect upon this engagement, Liberation Theology exists. Its continuation is a sign that prophecy is alive within the Church; that it has not forgotten the poor; and that the Gospel is still a force for good for the oppressed and the outcast. If we lose such values, we lose the theological meaning of the Christian community.

Liberation Theology is facing a new challenge: galloping and intransigent globalisation. It is imperative that we leave no stone unturned in counteracting its power and influence and that we seek to go beyond the mere economic controls which it exerts over the world in general and the Third World in particular.

Globalisation is an 'anthropogenic' trend. The words 'cosmos' and 'anthropology' have been replaced by 'cosmogenesis' and 'anthropogenesis', embodying an ongoing process of human evolution. Human beings have an innate drive to wander the earth, adapting to ecosystems as varied as the glaciers of the Antarctic to the parched regions of the Sahara. In this sense, globalisation is inherent in the human condition. The drive towards globalisation began in 1521 when Ferdinand Magellan circumnavigated the world: from then to the present, the world has undergone a gradual process of westernisation. Western culture succeeded in imposing its approach to nature through science and technology, its way of organising society (representative democracy), its view of the human person (the citizen's inalienable rights) and its way of understanding God (Christianity).

This process did not take place peacefully. The greatest ethnocide in history took place during the Spanish invasion of Mexico and Peru. Africa was colonised and completely destructured. The Far East suffered an enormous impact from the West's military and economic strength. This was the Iron Age of globalisation. But it laid the foundation for the globalisation we experience today and which manifests itself in the economic, political and spiritual spheres of human existence.

Economic and political processes go hand in hand. The West has practically forced the peoples of the Earth to organise themselves into nation states. Democracy has filtered into the psyche of nearly all countries, either as a universal value in human relationships, or as a form of organisation of state power. Democracy can only work in an atmosphere of respect for, and promotion of, collective human rights. Human rights, in turn, presuppose an understanding of humans as an end in themselves and never the means to an end. In the light of the universal validity of human rights, all power must be bound by a constitution and controlled by the people, or their representatives. The great World Wars and, in particular, the Gulf War of 1991 illustrate the adverse effect of the globalisation process.

Three factors have made globalisation an obvious reality: the communication process; the threat of nuclear destruction; and concern for the Earth's ecology. Communications have made us all neighbours. As a result of the media revolution, mankind will never be the same again. Nuclear and chemical weapons can destroy mankind: all humans can degenerate and perish. The ecological alarm was sounded by the Club of Rome in 1972 when it reported that the type of industrial development adopted by humanity involved a systematic assault on nature, a run-down of non-renewable resources and a huge deterioration in the quality of life of all living beings. We now have concrete evidence of ecocide (destruction of the ecosystem), biocide (extinction of living species) and geocide (extinction of the Earth-Gaia).

Globalisation can also manifest itself within the realm of spirituality. Economic, political and sociological factors give rise to another determinant of globalisation: a new planetary awareness. We are co-responsible and co-accountable for our common destiny, for the destiny of human beings and of the Earth. Indeed, human beings are one with the Earth, making up a sole entity with it. For the first time in the history of anthropogenesis, we have been able to see the Earth from outside itself. This is the vision of the astronauts, a vision which changes people's awareness. Russell Scheickhart testified to the change in one's mental 'landscape' on returning to Earth:

'When seen from the outside, the Earth is so small and so fragile it's a tiny, precious speck, which can be covered with the thumb. Everything which means anything to anyone, the whole of history, art, birth, death, love, joy and tears, all of this is to be found in that blue and white dot which can be covered with one's thumb.'

Human beings do not simply inhabit the Earth. They are Earth. As the Argentine poet Atauhalpa Ypanqui says: 'Man is the Earth that walks, the Earth that thinks, speaks and loves.' If life and non-life were in opposition, we would have the mechanical world on the one hand, and the biological and human world on the other, separated by impassable barriers. Earth sciences show that such barriers do not exist. Matter cannot be seen as static, but something which is characterised by reactivity, creativity and dialogue.

Modern cosmology spreads this vision throughout the world and leads us to understand that the universe represents an immense evolutionary process 15 billion years old. The arrow of time points in one direction: the appearance of ever more complex orders of life and creative expression. This perception of things provides the empirical and scientific basis necessary to understand the present-day process of globalisation as a moment within an immense ongoing process which has been at work in the universe from the beginning of time.

Globalisation, as Teilhard de Chardin might have put it, is laying down the conditions for a qualitative leap forward in the process of anthopogenesis: the irruption into our existence of the noogenesis and the noosphere; the genesis and the sphere of the spirit. We might witness a greater unity, a new history of the universe and a more supportive and fraternal human species. This awareness, slowly becoming worldwide, creates a new spirituality; one which is not so much a religious, but a human, attitude of veneration for the grandeur of the universe and the complexity of life on Earth.

Human beings are becoming more aware that they can become more receptive to the messages which come from all things. For persons of faith, the depths of the universe are inhabited by God and to converse with this inner depth is to be attuned to the divine Word. Throughout the world we see an increasing thirst for spirituality, for an encounter with that lost link which allows us to experience the reintegration of all things, giving sense to life, which is the truth of all religion.

What are the challenges for Latin American Liberation Theology? Liberation Theology sees globalisation as a sign to be interpreted. It is a stage in the cosmogenic and anthropogenic process and, as such, for believers, a sign of God's plan. Human beings are essentially made of an interweaving of relationships: globalisation enables them to fulfil their vocation in a more radical way than in any previous epoch.

In the prophetic dimension, Liberation Theology poses a further question: Where do the poor fit into the process? Economically, globalisation occurs according to the demands of capital. Because capital favours the private approbation of profits and the maximisation of returns, economic globalisation takes place to the exclusion of the masses. We are told that, during the 25 years (1965-1990) when the globalisation process began to accelerate, global wealth increased tenfold whilst the planet's population only doubled. During the same period, the share of wealth appropriated by the rich countries increased from 68 to 72 per cent whilst their population share decreased from 30 to 23 per cent of the world total.

Such a distortion shows that this type of market is profoundly anti-social. It does not produce according to human needs, but according to the demands of the market itself. We are not against a market which would be a central institution in modern society. We cannot, however, accept a market that is lethal to the majority of humankind. Given that world hunger is on the increase, if we wish to survive we shall be forced to change the nature of the world economy. It can no longer be seen solely in terms of material, linear and unchecked growth, but as a means to meet the needs of all humans and of other beings of creation.

Politically, Liberation Theology has serious reservations concerning the homogenisation of mankind through the generalisation of western values. Our task is to support multicultural and multi-religious societies, respecting their various forms of social and political organisation, based upon their respective cultures. The major challenge consists in managing forms of coexistence which exclude nobody. This can be achieved if the four essential supports of social life are present: sharing, the quest for equality, fellowship and respect for differences.

As for globalisation in the sphere of spirituality, theologians are convinced that not only the oppressed, but all humans must be liberated. We all live enslaved under a paradigm that makes us enemies of, and separates us from, nature. Not only the poor are crying out. The Earth cries out against our systematic assault upon it. Liberation Theology urges the recovery of the sacred character of the Earth and the preservation of the spiritual traditions of the oppressed cultures which, in general, honour the Earth as the Great Mother. This attitude may help create boundaries to modern greed and make possible a new experience of God which could overcome western Christianity's dualism between God and the world, soul and body, the feminine and the masculine.

Liberation theologians are convinced that only a Christianity which breaks off its alliance with the power of this world, relativises its embodiment in Western culture and takes up the cause of the wretched of the Earth – now two thirds of mankind – will be able to claim the inheritance of Jesus. A Chistianity of domination is of no use to globalisation. Globalisation will benefit from a Liberation Christianity which helps to create a type of globalisation which seeks harmony in diversity, not only in economic, polical and cultural terms but in religious ones as well. ❏

Leonardo Boff *is professor of ethics and philosophy of religion at the State University of Rio de Janeiro and is the author of more than 40 books on Liberation Theology. In 1985, the Congregation for the Doctrine of the Faith took exception to his criticisms of the Holy See in* Church: Charism and Power, *imposing a year of 'penitential silence' upon him. After pressure from Rome to suppress his theological activity, he gave up his ministry in 1992 and left the Franciscan order. Translated by Francis and Carol Pimentel-Pinto*

PETER CLARKE

In pursuit of the millennium

Apocalyptic cults and messianic religions are mushrooming in Brazil's seething urban slums and deprived Indian areas

Though associated in the popular mind with Catholicism, Brazil has a vast range of alternative and new religions, many of which derive from the interaction of African, Amerindian, Christian, Japanese Buddhist and Shinto and Spiritualist sources. The divinities worshiped not only reveal to their devotees their path in life, but provide them with models for living our their destinies. This is particularly true of Afro-Brazilian religions, which in Brazil take the two main forms known as *Candomble* and *Umbanda*.

A common feature of New Religious Movements (NRMs) in Brazil is the number of messianic movements, some more typically millennial than others. These include the Church of World Messianity (*Sekai Kyusei Kyo*), the Institute for Research in Human Happiness (*Kofuku no Kagaku*) and *Mahikari*, all from Japan, and the Unification Church (the 'Moonies') from Korea via the USA. Virtually all the movements of Asian and North American origin found elsewhere in the world are present in Brazil.

Indigenous movements are also numerous and include the Blue Butterflies (*Borboletas Azuis*), yet another messianic movement founded in 1961 by Roldao Mangueira (alias Padre Cicero), a former cotton merchant. A more practical kind of messianic religion has arisen in the form of the Brotherhood of the Holy Cross, initiated in 1972 by Brother Joseph of the Cross, among the Indian Tikuna and their neighbours of European descent in the Amazon region.

The Blue Butterflies movement and other Spiritist-inspired NRMs include the millennial *Legiao da Boa Vontade* (Legion of Good Will), founded in Rio in the late 1960s by José de Paiva Netto. This Spiritist NRM, for which the Biblical *Book of the Apocalypse* is the most important of scriptures, has attempted to reflect the ethnic diversity and religious pluralism of Brazil by building a large ecumenical Temple of Good Will with a pure crystal tower – to symbolise the unification of nations, cultures and races – and a World Parliament of Ecumenical Fraternity in Brasilia.

Several large and influential Protestant evangelical NRMs have emerged since 1950; one of the fastest-growing is *Igreja Universal do Reino de Deus* (IURD), founded in Rio do Janeiro in 1977 by Edir Macedo Bezerra, Bishop Macedo. The IURD is an urban phenomenon and, according to one expert, the crucial factor in explaining its success in the vast urban conglomerates of Latin America, such as São Paolo, is self-government. Those who join are 'able to devise their own social world for themselves'.

Such movements are extremely intolerant and opposed, in particular, to any kind of interaction with African-derived religion which they condemn as evil and practise exorcism on those who have participated in their activities. However, the competition for members is driving even fundamentalist, evangelical churches like the IURD into forms of syncretism it would never have tolerated a decade ago. In a bid to compete with the Catholic Church, it has, for instance, introduced a rival pilgrimage to the shrine of *Nossa Senhora de Aparçeida* in the state of Minas Gerais, the most popular religious pilgrimage in the country.

The interaction of African, Amerindian and Catholic beliefs, on the other hand, is commonplace. Well known examples include the tradition of *Candomble*, found mostly in Bahia in the Northeast, and known as *Xango* in Recife, *Batuque* in the northern state of Para and, in its more spiritualist form, as *Umbanda*, practised in Rio do Janeiro and São Paolo. While *Umbanda* also flourishes in Argentina and Paraguay, it has largely been overtaken by Cuba's *Santeria* or Haitian Voodoo in the migrant Brazilian communities of Los Angeles, Miami, New York and other North American cities.

Spiritism, particularly the tradition started in the nineteenth century by the Frenchman Hippolyte Rivail (1804-1869), alias Allan Kardec, has widespread appeal deriving from its desire to unite Christians and Spiritists and its emphasis on the spiritual roots of sickness. Kardec's ideas were widely promoted through the writings of the Brazilian Adolfo

Followers of 'Tia Neiva', Brazil – Credit: Rex/Sipa

Bezzera Menez de Cavalcanti. More recently, Francisco Candido Xavier, particularly through his 'psychographed' treatise *Nosso Lar* (Our Home), has done much to promote the Spiritist cause. *Nosso Lar*'s continuing appeal lies in its millennialism: the title of the treatise itself is the name of the as yet incomplete celestial colony reserved for Brazilians that the Portuguese founded in the sixteenth century and which is situated directly above Rio.

Outside the strict evangelical churches, it is rare to find an NRM that does not contain some influence from at least several of its religious traditions and this is also the case of the Santo Daime healing movement, which is becoming increasingly known in the US, Europe and Japan. Its essential spiritual roots derive from the *Tambor de Minas*, the largely Yoruba-based form of African-Brazilian religion practised in the northern state of Maranhao, and the ritual drinking of *ayauasca*, common to the indigenous peoples of the Amazon. The substance was given the name Santo Daime by the movement's founder, the shaman Irineus.

Japanese NRMs constitute the majority of non-indigenous NRMs, where they now number more than 30. Most are Buddhist in content, Shinto in ritual, Christian-influenced in much of their teaching. Movements such as *Seicho no Ie* (House of Growth) and *Seakai Kyusei Kyo* have attracted hundreds of thousands of members.

There are also a large number of thoroughgoing Shinto movements, two of the largest being the *Nambei Daijungu* (Great Sanctuary of Latin America) and the Shinto *Ikyo Daijinmeigu* (Great Shinto Sanctuary of Brazil), both of which are dependent on the *Ise Jingu* shrine at Ise where the cult of Amaterasu Omikami, the Great Goddess of the Sun, is said to have started. ❏

Peter Clarke is a professor of the history and sociology of religions and director of the Centre for New Religions at King's College, London

AUGUSTO BOAL

Give us back our torture house

In a successful plea to the Rio Chamber of Deputies, Brazil's most famous agit-prop dramatist called for the conservation of the apparatus of torment

However hard I might try – and I confess that I have never made the slightest effort to do so – I have never managed to make believe that I do not exist. I have never managed to pass through the world unnoticed nor make myself invisible. What I am going to say might seem threatening, but when anyone looks in my direction they always see a man. A man who exists.

My identity is formed from that which I am and that which I want to be. But it is also formed from that which I have been: I am the person I have been – my identity is also formed from my past.

A while back, the paper *O Globo* wanted to tell its readers of my origins, my childhood. I have been a baker, I've baked a lot of bread; many people have eaten bread I made with my own hands. *O Globo* took me back to my father's bakery in Penha where, in times gone by, I used to bake bread and sometimes serve at the counter, and they took my photo there. When I was myself in front of the oven, my friend for a good 10 years of my life, a wonderful part of my life came flooding back to me – to remember is to live, as the song has it. I remembered, I re-lived, I lived.

But I am not made of happy bread-baking memories alone. Sometimes I remember when I was a guerrilla. This is also part of me. It is my past, what I have been, what I am. Today I think it was a mistake. An honest mistake made by honest people, decent people like myself.

I have always been a believer in the rule of law and I am proud to belong today to this House, in which laws are made, which I promise to respect. As a believer in the rule of law, I never accepted the dictatorship. If I fought against it, I fought against subversion. The subversives were those who subverted the law and overthrew a perfectly legitimate regime. It was they who initiated the wave of kidnappings, the invasions of people's homes – they taught the wrongdoers who proliferate today. In my own case, for instance, I was never arrested; I was kidnapped by the São Paulo police. Me, whose only crime was to defend the law. The law which had been violated.

I was picked up in São Paulo and, like everyone else, I was tortured. But, as happens in the great Shakespearean tragedies, the most painful scenes are juxtaposed sometimes with scenes of ridiculous farce. A scene of torture is a scene of inhuman tragedy. But the infinite bestiality of the seven orangutans who tortured me – their incomparable ignorance – created an absurd dialogue of the deaf.

Among these seven mastodons, there was one who tried to justify everything with bureaucratic arguments. While he was giving me electric shocks on the *pau-de-arara,* from which I hung naked, upside down, he said: 'You will forgive me, yeah? But I am torturing you because it's on my schedule, see? I don't have anything personal against you, honest. I'm even a fan of your plays. I haven't seen any, but I like them all, see? You know how it is, yeah? Here you do what you're told to, see? Now, you know, it's a funny old world, things change. One day it might be you who's on top and me underneath, yeah? Now if it came to that, right, you're obviously not about to forget that I tortured you, fair enough, but it was just the luck of the draw, see? I tortured you because it was on my schedule.'

This was one of the mental defectives who punished me. There were others, of all kinds, of all races and pedigrees. The leader of the team, for instance, did not know why I was there, as the team that did the torturing was not the same as the team that did the kidnapping. They were specialised: each knew how to carry out his own particular crafts. Some made instruments of torture; others paid our country's foreign debt. All were acting in concert against a single victim – the Brazilian people.

It was then, when the pain was most intense, that I tried to engineer a break in the torment and I asked: 'What is it that you want me to confess?' I wanted a break but I had decided never to confess anything –

and I never did. But I wanted to buy time, so I asked him: 'What is it you want me to confess?'

At first the dinosaur did not know what to answer. He didn't know why he was torturing me – just that it was on his schedule. But the leader of the kidnap team had given him a list of accusations, written on a scrap of paper. He scanned the piece of paper and read out the first accusation: 'Boal, when you go abroad, you defame Brazil!' Me, defame Brazil! When I never tire of extolling the natural beauties of Baia da Guanabara. 'In what way do I defame Brazil?' I asked, hanging naked on the *pau-da-arara*. Reading on, the boor answered: 'You defame it because, when you travel, you tell people abroad that there is torture in Brazil.'

It did not register with the blockhead that he was doing just that, he was torturing me. The situation was so unreal, so funambulatory, that I laughed. When he saw me laughing, at first, he could not believe it – no-one laughs when they are hanging from the *pau-da-arara*! Then he became indignant, and turned the crank to increase the electric charge and asked why I was laughing. I answered that his present activity justified my past statements: in Brazil people are tortured, methodically and cruelly, and I was the living proof of it, strung up by my ankles, there, at that very moment. In one of the few moments of lucidity of his entire life, he thought, he thought very hard and ended up agreeing: 'You're right. I am torturing you. But since you are an artist, since you are well-known and you appear on television from time to time, I am torturing you, I give you that, but I am torturing you with respect.'

This episode in my life is part of me. I would like to go back to that cellar, where my only companion was a mouse, who was even more frightened than I was; I would like to see those instruments of torture again, those deadly but efficient tools. To revisit that building. I would like to re-see my past, to re-feel it, to re-live it. But the building, where episodes such as this took place has been destroyed. In its place, in São Paulo, they have constructed a supermarket. They have destroyed the memory. And without memory, imagination is impossible – without remembering, one does not imagine!

Without the past, the future would not exist and we would live like animals, ruminating on the present like cows. Let us not be cows. In São Paulo, because the memory of past atrocities has been destroyed, 111 prisoners were cruelly and premeditatedly cut down in Carandiru. The prisoners launched a revolt, the chief of police gave them an ultimatum, and then ordered the raid on the prison and the slaughter which resulted, coldly conscious of the crime he was committing. On a lovely Sunday evening, the horrors of the dictatorship came back to haunt us.

I appeal to my colleagues who are, like me, involved in the business of making laws, just as I used to make bread. I appeal to them to allow me to continue existing, so that a part of myself survives my death. The Vila Isabel house holds the memories of hundreds of men and women, it holds many stories, it holds History. Living History. Many of the men and women who were imprisoned there are today in these galleries watching us, just as I am on this platform looking at you. Those who are here today, they and I, we remember, and the past lives in our memory, which is part of our being. ❏

Augusto Boal *is a theatre director, dramatist, writer and teacher. Founder of the international movement* 'Theatre of the Oppressed', *he was MP for Rio de Janeiro from 1993 to 1996. This is an edited extract from a speech to the Assembly. It is in his latest book,* Legislative Theatre: Using performance to make politics *(Routledge 1998)*

JOSE EDUARDO AGUALUSA

Our cousins do not know us

An Angolan novelist 'discovers' black Brazil

I took a taxi one afternoon in Recife, in northeast Brazil. I was with an Angolan writer, Jackes dos Santos, the cultural attaché of the Angolan Embassy and a Brazilian historian friend of mine. On the following day, the taxi driver encountered my friend's husband in Olinda and he immediately informed him: 'Yesterday I transported your wife and three foreigners who were trying to speak Portuguese.'

Travelling inland, in the middle of Catinga, the rough, dry landscape where the gang of the famous bandit Lampiao wandered 70 years before, transforming himself into a popular hero, I met a girl who was incapable of understanding my questions. I repeated them in exactly the same words, while I made an effort to imitate the musical accent from the northeast, and her face lit up with a smile: 'I understand now. Why did you speak in a foreign language if you can speak Portuguese?'

Still in Brazil, this time in Rio de Janeiro, another taxi driver found my accent strange:

'Where do you come from?' I said I was from Angola. 'Angola?' he said with surprise, 'Where in Brazil is that?' When I explained to him that in Angola, a country with a population of 11 million, located in the western African on the other side of the Atlantic Ocean the language is also Portuguese, he was even more surprised: 'Really? I thought Portuguese was only spoken in Brazil.'

These incidents illustrate the relative cultural autism and, in particular, the lack of information average Brazilians have about Africa. It is a perverse ignorance: Brazil is clearly a nation of African origin. Black people, though, are still being associated with slavery and poverty; and they themselves have an inclination to deny their origins.

There may already have been African people among Pedro Alvares Cabral's sailors, who almost 500 years ago caught sight of the green hills of Brazil – or rather that which would later become Brazil. African people and their African descendants participated in the structuring process of Brazilian nationality from the beginning. It is not by chance that those expressions of Brazilian culture that projected the country abroad are essentially of African origin: popular music, carnival, *capoeira* or the powerful literary universe of Jorge Amado. The founders of Brazilian literature in the nineteenth century, notably Machado de Assis, Cruz and Sousa, were sons or grandsons of slaves.

Nevertheless, without noticing that it is a way of submitting once again to the power of prejudice, Afro-Brazilians prefer to turn towards the USA in search of a black identity of which they can feel proud, rather than look to Africa. We have witnessed for many years now the importation of concepts wildly at odds with Brazilian reality. What is even more ironic, some of those concepts are also out of synch in the USA, a country which, with several centuries delay, is beginning to be transformed, like all of Latin America, into an immense Creole nation. Recent studies indicate that in the next century most North Americans will be of mixed race. A growing number of Afro-American intellectuals have been supporting the study of Creole societies in Latin America in search of a model for their own future.

The visibility of black people in Brazil is sharply reduced in comparison with the USA. Although, according to the general assessment, most Brazilians are of African descent, the country shown through television looks astonishingly white. I have spent the last few months in Brazil working on the screen adaptation of my last novel, *Naçao Crioula* (Creole Nation). As a consequence of the war and the extreme dilapidation of Luanda, many of the scenes that take place in the Angolan capital at the end of the nineteenth century are to be filmed in one of the old colonial cities of Bahia. The apparently easy task of looking for black actors who could perform as Angolans, or slaves brought to Brazil, has proved in fact to be extremely difficult.

Angolans who visit Brazil show surprise and astonishment when confronted with the social invisibility of black people. The slaving system, which extended up to 100 years ago, and the lack of support programmes for the social improvement of slaves' descendants, in part explains this situation. Add to this the intense mixing of races and the arrival of a large number of European immigrants in the last decades, both leading to the 'whitening' of Brazilian society. In Angola, on the contrary, the trade in human lives allowed the emergence of an African enslaving bourgeoisie, relatively prosperous and powerful, whose descendants today control the political and economic power of the country.

Since there is no Spanish-speaking nation in that continent except for tiny Equatorial Guinea, Brazil stands out as the Latin American country in the best position to regain its links with Africa. There are five Portuguese-speaking countries in Africa, all originators of Brazilian identity and all, without exception, with their heart relatively open to Brazil.

Indeed, it needs to be reunited with Africa. While African music in Europe, for example, is gaining in popularity, renovating local traditions in France and Portugal, in Brazil nobody knows the Congolese composer Ray Lema, nor the Senegalese poet Leopold Senghor nor the Angolan painter António Ole. If they are to rebuild their pride and dignity, it is vital for Afro-Brazilians to re-discover the vitality of African culture. ❏

José Eduardo Agualusa is an Angolan novelist and author of A conjura (1989), Estação das chuvas (1996) *and* Nação crioula (1997). Translated by Alejandra Guibest

HG NETO AND CS SILVA

Vietnam

Once upon a time there was a marvellous city full of beaches,
squares and gorgeous women
A beautiful city glimpsed by the whole world – who doesn't
know the famous Rio de Janeiro?
The little tram up the hill, the Corcovado mountain, Christ
Redeemer
Copacabana Beach and the Flying Circus, pretty places that
attract the tourists
... of course the magazines only show what's suitable to see.
From our point of view, from the other side, there's bloodstains
on our postcards
On our postcards, rival gangs, brutal slaughter
That's why, amongst other reasons, there's no more tourists
here.
What goes on here and there has an impact across the
country
A fourth world inside a third, powder-keg ready to explode –
where's my lighter gone?
Carnage rules where the law's not in force, postcard of a future
that's already here
Welcome to São Paulo, welcome to Rio
Don't try to live for a day in Brazil's Vietnam

The Dutra highway links these two states, and in both there are
sleepless nights of worry
Under cover of impunity a lot of people die, good people, bad
people, innocent people
São Paulo and Rio are highly sought after, people leave their
homes and states

Looking for a job, easily duped – out there the South's a
beautiful place,
Here the South's just danger, out there the South's full of posh
folks,
Here the South's full of criminals, crowded with the rich and
poor, the poor and rich.
Welcome to São Paulo, welcome to Rio
Don't try to live for a day in Brazil's Vietnam

Law, authority and citizenship – fine words, that don't reach the
periphery of an unheard war
Just a battle – I remember the dates and find my memory
doesn't fail me
October 92, end of the year, and a while later I think again –
August 28 1993
It seems like a lie, they did it all over again, cruelty made into
an artform
And the states count the dead the following day – shotguns,
pistols, AR15
High-precision, high-calibre weapons, the banditry of the
police makes it all so easy
Criminal versus criminal in the crossfire, as long as impunity
speaks loudest
The blood from up on the hillside spills down onto the asphalt
Think twice before you come here, I feel I must alert your
attention
Welcome to São Paulo, welcome to Rio
Don't try to live for a day in Brazil's Vietnam

From Procurados – Vivos ou Mortos *by Pavilhão 9, Paradoxx Music, 1997.*
Translated by David Treece, director of the Centre for the Study of Brazilian
Culture and Society, King's College, London. He is currently researching the
black aesthetic in Brazilian culture and music, as part of a long-term book project
on Brazilian popular music

Saramago's voyage

Despite international recognition, Portugal's Nobel-winning author has always been an outsider

Until last month, the Portuguese writer José Saramago was widely read in Europe and Latin America but largely unknown in the Anglophone world. Whereas print runs in Portugal top 150,000, British and US publishers were hard put to produce over 3,000 for any of his novels. Winning the Nobel prize is set to change that but, for much of his career, Saramago has been a prophet largely unclaimed in his own land.

During the 1940s, he was a young radical. Under Europe's most durable fascist dictator, Salazar, a writer like Saramago was bound to suffer. Still a card-carrying member of the Communist Party, he also carries the authenticity of being born in a humble rural family, a grass roots proletarian. A photograph of his parents – father in a wellworn suit, mother in a floral dress, squinting into the sun behind the camera – adorns his study on the volcanic island of Lanzarote, a true place of isolation and exile.

Yet the reasons for remaining there are prosaic: his wife, the Spanish journalist Pilar del Río, had a brother living there, an architect who designed a house adjacent to his. It has since become a refuge, the one place where Saramago can write in privacy, overlooking the sea from a loft as high as a lighthouse and, in between, taking the dogs for great striding walks along the shore.

It wasn't ever so. Saramago was most persecuted when he was most consistently in Portugal. First as a political journalist and then as newspaper editor, he'd cut and duck to stay afloat. It was only after the death of Salazar in 1970 and the April Revolution that he suffered dismissal for his views. At this time of financial impoverishment the Portuguese *Circulo de Leitores* – a book club not dissimilar to *Readers' Digest* – proposed he write a chapter-by-chapter journey around Portugal, visiting not only the familiar cities and resorts, but also its more remote and architecturally challenging outposts.

Written in the serialised style of Dickens, *Viagem a Portugal* (Journey to Portugal) gives measured attention to each place and its circumstances, more like a diary than a travelogue. But a diary made anonymous by the use of the third person, his refusal to call the narrator anything other than 'the traveller'. When asked why he did so, he replied: 'I would have grown tired with all that "I – I – I".' But to render him anonymous is not to make him Everyman. On the contrary, the traveller is a man of strong opinions, who categorically prefers the Romanesque to the Baroque; Garrett and Castelo Branco to lighter-weight authors; *bacalhau* with potato rissoles to stew and dumplings; peasants to office workers; and the mountains to the plains.

Like all opinionated men, Saramago argues his views and winkles out the exceptions, mostly by communing with himself. But he is not averse to preaching about what he holds dear. Nor does being a militant atheist debar him either from argument with God or, acrostically, with Saint Anthony of Padua, through a variation of the latter's 'Sermon of the Fishes'. The well-travelled saint and the often saintly traveller, would probably have had much in common. Especially where the former's spiritual egalitarianism amd refusal to differentiate between the souls of beasts and mortals, meets the latter's Marxist internationalism, which refutes notions of the nation state as inappropriate to rivers, fish and humans alike.

Not that religious or political institutions have been more tolerant of Saramago than in the time of St Anthony. When *The Gospel according to Jesus Christ* was first published in 1991, the then Under-Secretary of State Sousa Lara warned against its 'unpatriotic undesirability'. Despite the more pragmatic reasons for Saramago's exile, he has since observed: 'It's true I went to live in Lanzarote as the result of a political problem, following the publication of a polemical novel I wrote. It was badly received in Portugal.' And not only in Portugal, where bookshops refused to stock it, but also in the Vatican, which voiced a cursory, but accurate, estimation of Saramago's 'largely anti-religious viewpoint'. This was followed up on 8 October 1998 when *L'Osservatore Romano* condemned Saramago's winning of the Nobel Prize for Literature as 'yet another ideologically slanted award' and, on more solid ground, that he is an 'unreconstructed communist'.

On receiving the award, Saramago declared himself 'not just happy for me personally but for my country', while noting that 'although the prize may not save Portugal from its present state of chaos, I believe it may, at least, foment greater interest in its writers'.

Now 75, with a lifetime of literary and political activity behind him, there are signs that Saramago is ready, if not for compromise, at least for reconciliation. Saramago has never fully forsaken political activism or literary criticism. He may no longer contribute to the *Diario de Lisboa* or *Serra Nova*; we are more likely to read articles justifying his intervention on behalf of the Chiapas rebels in *El Pais*, or his literary opinions in the serialised *Cadernos de Lanzarote*. And yet while he is now translated into 25 languages and Harvill continues to publish all his fiction, he remains unacknowledged at the highest level in his own land. Even as the Nobel Prize for Literature was bestowed in Stockholm, parliament in Lisbon refused to grant him honours as the greatest living Portuguese author. ❏

Amanda Hopkinson is a writer, journalist and translator, and a senior research fellow in the Department of Journalism, Media and Cultural Studies at the University of Wales, Cardiff

JOSE SARAMAGO

The Douro and the Duero

THE SERMON OF THE FISHES

Nothing of the kind had occurred within the living memory of a single border guard. This was the first traveller ever to pull up in his car, with the engine already in Portugal but the petrol tank still in Spain, and lean over the parapet at the precise point crossed by the invisible line of the frontier. Then, from across the deep dark waters, echoing between the tall rocky slopes on either side, the traveller's voice could be heard preaching to the fish in the River:[1]

'Gather round, fishes, those of you to the right still in the River Douro and those of you to the left in the River Duero, come closer all of you and advise me which language you speak when you cross the watery frontiers beneath, and whether down there you also produce passports and visas as you enter and depart. Here am I, gazing down on you from this high barrier, as you gaze back up at me, fishes residing in these mingling waters, and who can as easily find yourselves on one shoreline as on another, a grand fraternity of fishes who only devour one another for reasons of hunger and never on a patriotic impulse. Grant me, O fishes, clear instruction lest I forget this lesson on the second stage of my journey into Portugal: may I learn, in passing from one land to the next, to pay the closest attention to the similarities and differences, whilst not forgetting something common to both humans and fish alike, namely that a traveller has preferences and sympathies unconstrained by the obligations of universal love, never hitherto required of him. To you, then, I at length bid farewell, O fishes, until a future day: may you follow your own course out of the sight of fishermen. Swim joyfully on, and wish me a safe journey. Farewell, farewell.'

This was a fine miracle with which to start the journey. A sudden breeze ruffled the waters, or perhaps it was simply the disturbance caused by the submerging fish, for no sooner had the traveller fallen silent than there was nothing to be seen apart from the river and its shores, and nothing to be heard above the dozy hum of the car engine. That's the problem with miracles: they last such a short time. But the traveller is not a professional miracle-worker, he works them only by accident, so by the time he returns to his car he is already resigned to the fact. He knows he is about to enter a country rich in supernatural pageantry, as immediately witnessed by the first town he comes to in Portugal, one called Miranda do Douro,[2] which he enters in the precise fashion of the fastidious traveller. Here he is forced to recognise his own shortcomings, and admit he has everything to learn. About miracles, as all else.

It's an October afternoon. The traveller opens a window in the room where he is to spend the night and, at first glance, discovers or recovers the certainty that he is fortunate indeed. He could have faced onto a wall, a miserable piece of stonemasonry, or an area strung with washing, and have had to content himself with the sense of utility, of decay, or simply the hygiene of a washing line. But what he encountered was the stony bank of the Spanish Duero, so hard in its composition that even brushwood could scarcely find a hold and, since strokes of luck never occur singly, the sun was positioned in such a way as to create an enormous abstract painting in varying shades of yellow, tempting him to remain there staring for as long as there was still light. At this point in time the traveller doesn't yet know that a few days hence he'll be in Braganca, in the Abade de Bacal Museum, staring again at the same stone, maybe even at the same shade of yellow, only here in a painting by Dordio Gomes. No doubt he will be shaking his head and muttering: 'It's a small world....'

In Miranda do Douro, for example, it is impossible to get lost. Descend the Rua da Costanilha, with its fifteenth-century houses, and we're hardly aware of the city gates but are already out beyond the town, overlooking the vast valleys stretching to the west. We are shrouded in a heavy medieval silence: what a strange period to find ourselves in, and what a strange people to be among. To one side of the gateway huddles a group of women, all dressed in black, speaking in low voices; not one of them is still young – few of them, in all probability, can remember ever having been so. The traveller, as you would expect, has a camera slung over his shoulder, but feels embarrassed, still unaccustomed to the boldness customarily adopted by tourists, which is why there's no pictorial record of those shadowy women who have been talking there since the world began. The traveller has a melancholic sense of foreboding that a journey which commences thus will come to a bad end. He falls into a brown study, happily only for a few moments then, near at hand, just beyond the walls, he hears the roar of a bulldozer engine, levelling a new high road: progress at the gates of the Middle Ages.

He climbs back up the Costanilha, turning off into other roads and side streets. There's no-one at any of the windows, only traces of ancient anti-Spanish rancour in the form of obscene graffiti scored into good fifteenth-century stone. This therapeutic scatology, which runs no risk of offending either the eyes of a child or the most turgid of our defenders of morality, made him want to laugh.

In five hundred years nobody had bothered to get the offending slogans effaced or excised, inescapable proof that the Portuguese don't lack a sense of humour, merely that they only exercise it in the service of their patriotic interests. This was not the place to learn the lesson of the fishes of the Duero, yet perhaps it had its own logic. If at the end of the day, heavenly powers favoured the Portuguese over the Spanish, it would look bad if the humans on this side were to override the interventions from on high and defy their authority. The story can be briefly told.

The struggles of the Restoration[3] were underway in the mid-seventeenth century and Miranda do Douro, here on the banks of the Duero was, so to speak, no more than a stone's throw away from enemy assaults. The city was besieged, hunger was widespread, those laid siege to weakened, and, for a time, Miranda seemed lost. It was at this point, so the story goes, that a child appeared, rallying the flagging populace to arms, infusing them with spirit and courage where courage and spirit were flagging, so that in no time they cast off their faintheartedness and low spirits, seized genuine or improvised weapons, and followed the boy against the Spanish like a herd trampling the new-grown corn. Seeing their enemy thrown into confusion, Miranda do Douro triumphed, and another famous page was inscribed in the annals of those wars. Only – where was the commander of the victorious army to be found? Where that gentle combatant who had exchanged a spinning top for a field marshal's baton? Nowhere to be seen, he couldn't be traced, indeed he was never seen again. Therefore, according to the populace of Miranda, it was a miracle. And therefore, it was additionally deduced, he must have been the Child Jesus.

So the traveller can confirm. If he could preach to the fishes, as they could listen to his sermon, he had no reason to disbelieve the ancient strategies of war. Still less so when actually confronted by the Child Jesus of Cartolinha, two handspans high, a silver sword at his waist, a red sash falling from his shoulder, a white bow at his neck and a cap perched on top of his rounded infantile head. This is hardly the uniform of victory, just one taken from an ordinary wardrobe, a regular and everyday outfit, as the Cathedral verger explained to the traveller. Well aware of his duties as a guide, the verger, on observing the scrupulous attention being paid by the traveller, brought him into a side-building housing a collection of various pieces of statuary, protected from the temptations of professional and amateur thieves alike.

Matters were now resolved. A small tableau, sculpted in high-relief, was the traveller's final proof of how much he has yet to learn where miracles are concerned. Here Saint Anthony is receiving the genuflexion of a sheep, offering an exemplary lesson in faith to the shepherd who had dared mock the saint, and there, in the sculpture, you can see the latter flushed with shame and therefore, by this very fact, capable of redemption. According to the verger, many still make mention of the picture but few actually visit it. You must forgive the traveller's utter inability to contain his vanity. He came from so far away, without the least introduction, and was admitted to these mysteries simply on account of his honest face.

The journey is but beginning and, meticulous as he is, the traveller immediately falls to questioning his motives. What kind of a journey is this after all? Simply a question of taking a turn about the town of Miranda do Douro, visiting the cathedral with its verger, its little capped child and the sheep, something that, once accomplished, he ticks off on his map, then hits the road again and says, like the barber shaking off his towel: 'So, on to the next!' A journey is supposed to be cast in a different mould, a matter more of being than moving on. Perhaps recognition should be given to the travellers' careers, but only for those with a genuine vocation, for the rest who believe in taking their responsibilities lightly are deceiving themselves: each kilometre is worth no less than a year of life. Wrestling with contemplations like these, the traveller ends up by falling asleep. When he awakes next morning there before him is the yellow stone, for ever in the same place as it is in the destiny of a stone to be, except if an artist should come to carry it away in his heart.

On the way out of Miranda do Douro, the traveller continues sharpening his powers of observation so that nothing may get lost and everything prove to be of benefit, and to this end he turns his attention to a little river running close by. As we've established rivers have names, and this one – so near to the abundant Douro – what name might it have? He who doesn't know, asks, and he who asks sometimes receives a reply: 'Excuse me please, but what is this river called?' 'This river is called Fresno'. 'Fresno?' Yes, sir, Fresno'. 'But *fresno* is a Spanish word that in Portuguese would be *freixo [fresh]*. Why don't you call the river Freixo?' 'Ah, that I can't tell you. It has always been called that, as far as I know.' So, at length, in spite of all the repeated struggles against the Spanish, despite even the divine interventions of the Child Jesus, we still have this Fresno ensconced between its pleasant banks, laughing at the traveller's patriotism. He remembers his fishes, the homily he delivered to them, amusing himself with the memories, until he reaches the village of Malhadas where his spirits begin to lift: 'Who knows if this *fresno* matter doesn't arise straight out of a Mirandese dialect?' It occurred to him to ask as much, but then he forgot, and when much later his doubts revived, he decided it was of no importance. In usage at least, *fresno* could now pass as Portuguese.

Malhadas is situated a little way off the main road that continues on to Braganca. Close at hand are the remains of a Roman road the traveller has no intention of following. But when he asks after it to a peasant and his wife whom he encounters on his way into the village, they tell him: 'Aha! what you mean is the Moorish high road'. So be it: the Moorish high road. All that presently interests the traveller is the why and wherefore of the tractor from which the worker dismounts with the familiarity of someone in charge of his own property. 'I own just a small plot of land. The tractor's too much for me alone. Sometimes I hire it out to my neighbours, and that's how I manage to stay ahead.' The three of them pause to chat, discussing the problems that beset parents with children to maintain, and it soon becomes apparent that there's another one on the way.

When the traveller announces his intention of heading for Vimioso before returning by the same route, the peasant woman, without pausing to seek her husband's permission, invites him in, saying: 'We live in that house over there. Come and eat with us.' It was obviously a genuine invitation, meaning that however much (or little) there were in the pot, it would be unequally divided, since it's more than certain that the traveller would find the bigger and better part of it on his plate. The traveller thanked them, postponing the occasion. The tractor sets off, the woman retires to the house. 'They're real merrymakers in that village', she'd added, so the traveller took a turn around it which had hardly begun before it was brought to a halt by the spectacle of the giant black tortoise of the parish church with massive walls and hefty flying buttresses forming the creature's feet.

In the thirteenth century and in these the lands of Tras-os-Montes, locals could have known little of the resistance of the materials they employed, or perhaps the builders had renounced all trust in the certainties of this world and determined to construct for all eternity. The traveller entered and surveyed the belfry and the roof, letting his eyes run over them and into the distance, more than a little intrigued by a trans-mountainous land that fails to collapse into the abrupt precipices and valleys his imagination was fabricating. Ultimately it has to be each to its own: this was undeniably a plateau, and the traveller was not going to gainsay his fantasy, particularly given how useful it had proved in transforming the church into a tortoise: only a fellow visitor can judge just how fair and correct such a comparison really is. Two leagues further on lies Cacarelhos. Here, Camilo Castelo Branco[4] tells us, Calisto Eloi de Silos was born and Benevides de Barbuda, Agra de Freimas' eldest son, the rustic hero and the glutton in *Queda dum Anjo*, a novel of considerable humour and a certain melancholia. The traveller estimated the aforementioned Camilo could not escape the censure acidly proffered by Francisco Manuel do Nascimento, in accusing him of making fun of Samarda, as others had before, at the expense of Macas de D. Maria, Ranhados or Cucujaes. In linking Eloi with Cacarelhos the place had been subjected to ridicule, or maybe this only serves to demonstrate our own spiritual defects in preferring to apportion blame to the land and not to those the land produces. The apple rots according to the ailment of the apple tree, and not from the sickness of the earth. It goes without saying that the worst ailment of this village was its remoteness, here at the world's back-end, and it's unlikely that its reputation has much to do with what those in Minho mutter amongst themselves: for the people of Cacarelhos are gossips, incapable of keeping a secret.

Cacarelhos must have its secrets but nobody revealed any to the traveller when he arrived on a local market day to encounter herds of beautiful honey-coloured cattle, eyes like lifebuoys of tenderness, lips white as snow ruminating in peace and serenity while a thread of saliva slowly dribbles down, all this beneath a forest of lyres, their carapace of horns, natural sound-boxes for the lowing which, from time to time, rise from the candelabra'ed company. Clearly there are secrets in all this, but not the kind to be related in words. It's easier to keep counting the banknotes, so many for this ox, take the beast with you, you won't regret your choice.

The chestnut trees are coated in prickly bobbles, so many that they look like flocks of greenfinches pausing to collect their strength, gathering in their branches ready for great migrations. The traveller is a sentimentalist. He stops his car and picks a prickly sweet chestnut as a simple reminder for many months to come. Now it has dried out, it must be time for him to return and visit the great chestnut tree beside the main road, relishing again the bright morning air culminating in a definite rural promise of chestnuts.

The main road twists and turns towards Vimioso and the contented traveller murmurs: 'What a beautiful day'. There are clouds in the sky, white fluffy ones which cast scattered shadows over the countryside; a light wind blows; the world looks newborn. Vimioso is built on a gentle slope, a placid little town, or so it seems to the passing traveller who has no intention of staying there, only of requesting some information from a woman he sees. But here he encounters his first disappointment. His informant is very friendly, to the extent of showing willing to take a turn around the backstreets and show him the local specialities, but what she really wants is to sell him her hand-stitched linen. Please don't take this amiss, but the traveller holds to his principles and persists in his conviction that the world is obliged to provide him with nothing beyond the information he is requesting. He descended a steep street down to the bottom, where he met his reward. To his eyes, unfamiliar with the sacred architecture of the countryside, there was no small pleasure to be found in the contrast between the robust seventeenth-century facades and the incipient signs of Baroque frigidity. The nave's interior was low and broad, Romanesque in a character not borne out by other architectural features. But the best was yet to come. Outside, under the trees' shade and seated on the steep stairway giving onto the courtyard, the traveller heard the story of the church's construction. In return for a private chapel, a certain family offered a pair of oxen to haul the stone intended for the church. The oxen devoted two years to the effort, pacing out the steps from the quarry to the outhouse used by the builders, whose part in the job ultimately amounted to no more than shouting 'giddy-up!' as the beasts came and went without either herdsman or guardsman, deafening the surrounding wasteland with the groans of badly greased blocks of stone, while profound discussions regarding the presumptions of men and their families raged. The traveller wished to know of the chapel and whether the original benefactors had descendants who continued to make use of it. Nobody could tell him. He found no particular marks of distinction within, although they might still exist. What does persist is the tale of a family who donated nothing of their own beyond the oxen who paid the price of their exhaustion, and in so doing opened up the way to guide their owners to paradise.

The traveller retraced his steps, distracted from the path now familiar to him. In Malhadas there was the temptation to claim the meal offered him earlier, but he held to his sense of timidity even though he suspected he would later repent of it. Instead, he went to where the *pauliteiros* dancers live in the village of Duas Igrejas. Since it was not the season for them to appear, the traveller never learnt any more about them than how the dancers took hours to slowly process through the streets. However, the traveller retains a right to his imagination and, as regards the matter of *pauliteiros*, it would then as now have been both more seemly and proper to alter the dance so that instead of crossing sticks the dancers use sabres or daggers. Then the Child Jesus of Cartolinha would have had sound military reasons for inspecting the army trooping in their embroidered ruffs and cravats. It's a defect of the traveller's: he wishes to improve on perfection. May the *pauliteiros* forgive him.

By the time he reaches Sendim, it's supper time. What and where should he eat? Someone recommends the traveller to: 'Follow this street onto the square, and in the square there's the Restaurant Gabriela. Ask there for Senhora Alicia'. Such informality is to the traveller's liking. The waitress informs him that Senhora Alicia is in the kitchen. The traveller looks through the doorway and a great smell of cooking fills the air as he inhales; a pot of greens is bubbling on the hob, while from across a heavy table in the centre of the room, Senhora Alicia asks the traveller what he would like to eat. The traveller is more accustomed to being brought a menu, to choosing as it were in the dark, and now he's obliged to order directly and Senhora Alicia suggests a fillet of veal, Mirandese-style. The traveller agrees and goes to sit at a table where, to make his mouth water, he is brought a tasty vegetable soup, accompanied by bread and wine. What is the fillet of veal going to be like? And why is it described as a fillet? A fillet has, to him, always meant a fillet of fish. 'Which country am I in?' the traveller asks his glass of wine, which fails to reply but genially permits him to continue drinking. 'There's not too much time for questions'. The gigantic chunk of veal comes swimming in vinegary gravy, cut down to the size of the plate so that it doesn't drip on the tablecloth. The traveller thinks he is dreaming. Soft flesh into which the knife cuts effortlessly, cooked to perfection, and that vinegary sauce which brings a sweat to the cheeks, the clearest proof that bodily contentment exists. The traveller is eating a meal in Portugal, his mind's eye filled with past and future landscapes, while Senhora Alicia can be heard shouting in her kitchen and the waitress giggles and shakes her plaits. ❑

José Saramago was awarded the 1998 Nobel prize for literature.
This excerpt from Viagem a Portugal *translated by Amanda Hopkinson*

---

[1] This is closely based on a famous sermon of St. Anthony of Padua (also claimed by the city of his borth, Lisbon), a 13th century Francoscam friar and doctor of the Church. Known as the 'Hammer of Heretics', his homilies were anthologised, including those addressed to birds, beasts...and fishes.

[2] Literally a belvedere over the Douro, whose name follows *ouro*, meaning gold, hence *douro*, a coin. Also *douro*, meaning dory, the fish. Whereas Duero, the Spanish version, is simply a name.

[3] The struggle to restore the Portuguese monarchy began on 1 December 1640 with an uprising against the Spanish king. Since 1580, Portugal had been ruled by the Spanish crown and only regained her independence through lengthy wars which lasted until 1668.

[4] Camilo Castelo Branco (1826–90) was an outstanding literary figure, situated between the traditions of romantic and realist writing. A passionate personality who went from one crisis of poverty to the next amorous scandal and confrontations with Oporto's commercial bourgeoisie. A pamphleteer in the style of Dumas, he left a legacy of 262 works.

BABEL

Forbidden histories

**Photographs and oral testimony from *Ukraine's forbidden history*
by Tim Smith, Rob Perks and Graham Smith**

Ukraine's declaration of independence on 24 August 1991
precipitated the disintegration of the Soviet Union and finally
unlocked tongues that had been silenced by decades of repression. From
remote country villages, towns and the industrial heartland in the east of
Europe's biggest new state this century, people gave voice to memories
and experiences hitherto recalled only among intimate family and
friends.

For three generations, since the Russian Revolution of 1917,
Ukrainians were forbidden to remember, let alone speak. As
organisations such as Memorial, created to investigate and commemorate
the victims if Stalin's repression, began to unearth the mass graves of his
victims in Ukraine, oral testimonies emerged to reconstruct a history
that had been so long denied.

Ukraine's lack of natural boundaries and physical obstacles has often
left it at the mercy of its more predatory neighbours: within living
memory, parts of what is now Ukraine (literally, 'borderland') have been
Polish, Romanian, Czech, Austro-Hungarian, Belarusian, German,
Russian and Soviet. The century has been a brutal one: Polish, German
and Soviet occupation of Ukraine took a huge toll in lives. Between
1930 and 1945 alone, approximately 15 million people, over a quarter of
the country's population, died as a result of famine, mass executions and
deportations, war and internal chaos as rival groups fought for control of
the country. Older people recall living through two world wars, a
revolution, a civil war, three famines, violent occupation by four armies
and deportation to Siberian labour camps.

By the 1920s, Ukraine was part of the Soviet Union, ruled directly from Moscow. Stalin's forced collectivisation of the land began in 1929. Intellectuals and wealthier peasants were labelled kulaks and shot or deported to labour camps, as were all who refused to join the collective farms or *kolkhoz*. Up to 10 million were deported; three million died in the camps. The subsequent collapse in agricultural production led to the Great Famine of 1932-33; as many as seven million starved to death, something the government went to great lengths to keep secret from the cities as well as the foreign press.

Hard on the heels of the famine came the Great Terror, a massive purge of every level of society in which people were randomly arrested, deported or summarily executed without trial, often for no other reason than the settling of private scores. Between 1935 and 1941, Stalin's secret service, the NKVD, arrested 19 million people; at least a million of the seven million who died were Ukrainians. Their bodies were dumped in secret graves, revealed only in the early 1990s with the help of survivors.

On 22 June 1941, Hitler broke his non-aggression pact with Stalin by invading Ukraine. Five-and-a-half million Ukrainians died including at least a million Jews in the course of World War II. By far the worst atrocity was the massacre at Babi Yar, a large ravine on the outskirts of Kiev: 33,771 Jews were murdered in two days; a further 70,000 bodies were added to the mass grave between 1941 and 1943.

Ukraine emerged from the war united but once again under Soviet rule; pre-war practices were resumed, organised dissent – by writers, historians, journalists – driven underground. By the late 1980s, opposition to Moscow crystallised around Soviet incompetence and lies in the face of the Chernobyl disaster; the deteriorating economy; and the high profile celebration of 1,000 years of Christianity in Ukraine. Released dissidents began to initiate debate on the atrocities of Soviet power. With independence in 1991, people were free to speak their mother tongue, worship in the church of their choice and rediscover a past that had been denied. It remains a contested history, seen from differing perspectives, but one to which all are now able to add their fragments of the truth. ❑

JVH

Circa 1930: a kulak family are forced to leave their home in the village of Udachanoya, near Donetsk, as part of Stalin's collectivisation of the land. Credit: Ukrainian State Archive

'Collectivisation began in 1929. The party representatives visited every house and if the family refused to join the *kolkhoz* they were deprived of their property and sent to Siberia. They took our cow even though we were 11 children in our family – little ones – and my mother kneeled down and begged the activists. About 30 families from our village were sent to Siberia. Some families who didn't want to join the *kolkhoz* were taken out of the village and thrown naked into the snow, and they froze to death.'

'By 1931, everyone was in the *kolkhoz*. Everyone worked hard but didn't get a salary, only credits in a book. The starvation began in the autumn of 1931: absolutely everything was taken out of the village. They came to every house to search for bread. If anyone tried to hide grain they took long poles and searched under the ground. People were hungry and they died. Laughter disappeared from the village. In spring 1932, people had to eat plants; there were no vegetables, no food at all, we had to eat leaves from the trees. 1933 was the worst: my whole family died. Only me and my little brother survived. It was a terrible time, terrible.'

1935: US newspaper report of the enforced famine in Ukraine. Credit: Ukrainian State Archive

SECOND SECTION
NEWS, FEATURES
SOVIET FAMINE
Animals Starve

'Stalin took everything from the people. The result was starvation – people were falling in the street. By 1933, all was gone and people were forced to go to the collective farm. My sister was asking my mother for something to eat, but there was no bread or milk. My sister wanted to eat her hands, so my mother tied her hands to her side.'

'I remember my little brother and sister: the first word they pronounced was not "mother", but "give, give, give" all the time. They faded very quickly. People began to eat people. There was a little church in our village and dead bodies were taken to it. When they came to take them to the cemetery they saw that some people had cut off a hand, a piece of the body, in order not to die of hunger.'

'There were attempts to leave but there were soldiers on all Ukraine's borders; it was impossible to get out. They killed everyone who attempted to go to other republics. In our village, 3,000 people died, compared to 185 who died later in the war.'

Kiev 1991: fiftieth anniversary of the Babi Yar massacre of the city's Jewish population. A man shows pictures of his family murdered at the ravine in 1941. This was the first official recognition of the event. Credit: Tim Smith

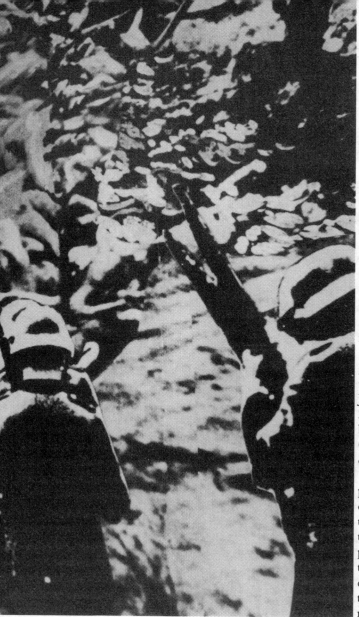

'When the Germans came we welcomed them with milk, bread, butter and eggs. The village was like a paradise with Germans offering cigarettes, chocolates, all the good that came from the West. The people could see that this was a different army altogether. So they cut up Ukrainian flags.'

'One day when I was going to school I had to step over dead Jewish bodies. Mothers holding babies killed by German drunkards during the night.'

'Ukrainian policemen formed a corridor and drove the people towards the glade, forced the people to undress and then go in the columns in twos and threes towards the mouth of the ravine ... on the opposite side there were the German's machine guns. Then the next hundred were brought. The policemen took the children by the legs and threw them alive down into the Yar. The Germans undermined the wall of the ravine and buried the people under thick layers of earth. But the earth was moving long after because wounded and still alive Jews were still moving. One girl was crying, "Mammy, why do they pour the sand into my eyes?"'

One of the exhumation carried out by Memorial, an organisation dedicated to uncovering past crimes of the Soviet system. Credit: Tim Smith

'The aim of the excavations is to gather information to begin court cases against the perpetrators. When we started digging in 1991 no-one would come up because everyone was afraid. After a month, some people came up to testify. We identified one man from his buttons, another by his shoes.'

'The main cause of death is violent murder, most of them being shot in the head.'

'We also help people find members of their family who were lost in World War II or were exiled to the Bolsheviks' camps where they disappeared. ... We also publish books of long forgotten Ukrainian authors.'

'People say there's no need to do the excavations but don't listen to them. People who don't understand say, "Why dig? Just make a grave and put a fence round it." But others who do understand say the world must know about this.'

'We open the hole; sometimes there are 16, 20 people in one hole. Sometimes it's hard to estimate how many people are there. We photograph the hole and every skeleton is taken out separately. It is washed, photographed again with a number and put in a box.'

1997: young men outside a church in Ivano Frankivsk. Credit: Tim Smith

'Ukraine's history was forbidden ... our art and literature has not been allowed to flourish. In 10 years things will change.'

'The church here did very well considering what it was up against, but it could not develop its intellectual life. Anything that needed books and texts, they were all confiscated and it could not be fostered.'

'The three big new factories that have opened here in this town make Coca-Cola, cigarettes and candy. I think we need more than that to live on.'

'At least we had some kind of insurance in Soviet times, now we have lost everything. We get by tending our chickens and gardens and sometimes we go into Donetsk selling eggs. But we haven't seen any butter or sausages here for months. I'm fed up eating potatoes. Thank God it's been raining and our gardens are doing well.'

'It's very difficult for people to change their mentality. But with the new generation, they've nothing from the old political system of the last 50 years. I'm an optimist about the future of Ukraine.'

Bykivnya forest on the outskirts of Kiev, secret burial ground of Stalin's Ukrainian victims. As late as 1988, Soviet authorities maintained bodies accidently found here were killed in World War II and erected a public monument to the 'victims of fascism'. Credit: Tim Smith

'Everyone who had their own opinion about life, it didn't matter who they were, maybe a writer or a worker or a member of a collective farm – they were repressed here ... They shot them in Kiev. We estimate that there are about 200,000 lying there but the KGB archives have, we think, been destroyed. The witnesses said that in this forest the lorries began to bring bodies as early as 1929. These were isolated incidences when soldiers would come at night, dump the bodies and cover them up. It was in 1936 when the repressions became more severe that they began to bring lorry loads here and they started a whole enterprise for killing ... Everyone knew that these were bodies that had been shot before the war, but they only spoke about it quietly as they were afraid ... For a long time, people wondered and we looked and guessed; then, in the 1960s, they began to talk about this place. Then, in the 1980s, the situation became more apparent. I come here every year. My grandfather lies here. He was shot in Kiev in 1936. Everyone knows someone here ... At the beginning of every May, people come and hold a meeting to the memory of those who were shot here. This year [1991], we announced that everybody who had lost a member of their family should come and place a piece of paper on the trees to announce they had lost someone here.' ❏

Ukraine's forbidden history by **Tim Smith, Rob Perks and Graham Smith** *is published by Dewi Lewis Publishing, 8 Broomfield Road, Heaton Moor, Stockport SK4 4ND, UK in association with Bradford Heritage Recording Unit, British Library National Sound Archive and University of Sheffield. ISBN 1-899235-56-6*

GALINA MASHTAKOVA

Left off the list of the human race

When the adult world is about its evil deeds it doesn't give a damn about the children

What I am writing about here is the aftermath of the last all-out attack on Grozny in August 1996. I was one of those who witnessed two 'Rooks' taking off every hour from Mozdok airfield to bomb the city. The refugees were mostly Russians, fooled by the promise of a 'safe corridor'. There was no such thing. Towards the end of August children began crawling out of the rubble. (The orphans left by the 1995 attacks had long since fled to who knows where.)

When the negotiations started between Alexander Lebed and Mohamed Talboev, I went back to Grozny. We began to gather children around the command centre, about 40 of them. This was the moment when prisoners of war were being exchanged for motorcycles, for flour, for dried milk. The goods were stored in a church, and we could get enough from there to boil up some wretched soup for the children at least.

I went to Moscow to organize the children's evacuation. I had no inkling of the scale of the problems I would encounter. Nobody, I was to discover, wanted these children. In Grozny everything had been bombed until there were no registry office records nor certificates left. In Russian terms, this meant that those concerned no longer had an identity. 'No ID, no identity, no problem for us to deal with': the old bureaucratic principle remains as valid as ever. I came back to Moscow, wrote a newspaper article, naturally, and was summoned to a meeting with Victor Ilyushin, the then first deputy prime minister.

There was a spring in my step as I set off to see him, the man at the

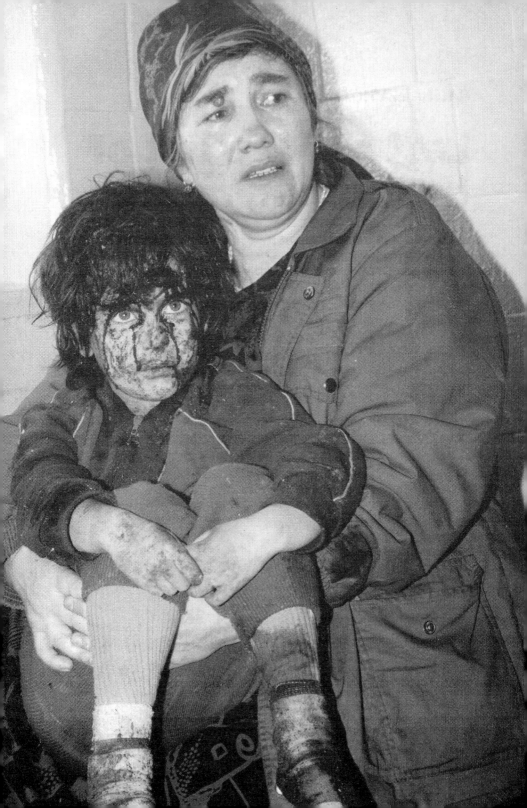

top! Everything would be sorted out in no time. But he greeted me with truly memorable words: 'Galina Nikolaevna, how are you? I have been looking forward all day to meeting you. This is so interesting. Are there really orphans in Grozny?' That did take the feet from under me. These people live by a logic quite divorced from the world the rest of us live in. When I said, 'Do you think you can bomb the place for two years and not make any orphans?' his aide gave me a sharp dig in the ribs as if to say, 'Remember who you're talking to'. Then Ilyushin gave a display of hyperactivity, but after five minutes he made me want to laugh. He has 35 telephones. He picked up a receiver and said, 'Anatoly Sergeivich, see to it that by tomorrow the name Mashtakova is known to everyone who counts in Grozny.' Over the two years of the war every last dog in Grozny had got to know me, whether it was Chechen or Russian. Well, all right, I thought, perhaps that's just their way of talking. He picked up another telephone: 'Sergei Kazhugetovich, do we have a plane available?' (To my knowledge Sergei Kazhugetovich had just sent two planes off to Iraq, so I was pretty sure he still had one to spare.) 'I've got a lady journalist here with me, and we need to send a plane urgently to evacuate orphans from Grozny.' To this Sergei Kazhugetovich naturally replied, 'Who has given permission for them to be evacuated?' Ilyushin turned to me: 'Galina Nikolaevna, who has given permission for them to be evacuated?' I said, 'Well, actually there is a bit of a difficulty there. I don't just need a plane. I've already spoken to Lebed, I've spoken to Rybkin, and they told me there would be no separate heading on children in the negotiations. At the moment they are more interested in getting a unified security system. So far I've got an offer of help from the Omsk OMON police team and one of the field commanding officers I know. It would be good if you could let me have Salavat (Kazhugetovich's head of security, whom I knew). He would be prepared to help me.' Whether Shoigu liked it or not, he wouldn't be able to go against the first deputy prime minister.

We flew out the next day at six in the morning. I couldn't believe my eyes. Our discussion had taken place at nine the previous evening, and by six o'clock the following morning there were 27 journalists sitting in the ministry's plane. When I came into the cabin I blurted out, 'What are you all doing here?' I couldn't help myself. I had thought we were going on quite a different mission. At that precise moment I felt least of all like a journalist. Our job was to evacuate children. Once they were

Chechen girl, wounded by Russian bombing, Chali, 1995 - Credit: East News/Sipa

out the newspapers could write whatever they liked. But no, the
Ministry for Crisis Situations had decided to do its good deed in the
spotlight. Twenty-seven journalists and one extra lady. 'How do you do,'
she said to me. 'My name is Margarita Nikolaevna. The Ministry of
Social Security has allocated me to rescue the children together with
you.' (Could they really not have found someone a bit younger and a bit
more mobile?) 'I have had lots of experience. We are going to take them
to Ossetia.' Everybody present gasped, 'Whe-ere?!' It was impossible to
imagine anything more disastrous and idiotic in the present
circumstances. Just at the very moment the entire Muslim world was
dead set against Ossetia, that was where we were going to evacuate
children from Chechnya. It would make no difference whether they
were Russian children or Chechen children: they simply would never be
allowed through to the border. Precisely because they were being sent to
Ossetia. Okay, so I lost my temper. Margarita Nikolaevna remonstrated
with me: 'My dear, do try to control yourself. I am much older than
you, and I really do have a great deal of experience. Back in 1960 I
helped evacuate children from the Tashkent earthquake to the Artek
children's village.'

We flew to Nazran where a car was waiting for me. I asked, 'Who
wants to come with me?' To see the children. 'No,' they said, 'first we
have to sort out where we are going to stay and how we are going to
eat.' 'Okay then,' I say, 'we'll sort everything out tomorrow over the
military telephone line.' I, Serezha Gerasimenko and the crew from the
Vzglyad news programme, went to Grozny. No word from the others the
next day, or the next. No sign of them in Grozny. You couldn't
accidentally drive past where we were without noticing: there was no
city left standing; there only was the command centre. I rang them.
Someone from the Ingushetia Migration Service told me, 'They haven't
got time. They are all too busy giving dozens of press conferences every
day. If we had just brought in the children straight away there would
have been no problem, you could have evacuated them to Russia
without anyone noticing, but now there's an almighty commotion. They
trumpeted from the rooftops to all of Ingushetia that they were going to
evacuate the children. It's a madhouse. They've really put us on the spot.
Shamil took me by the scruff of the neck and held me for two days at
the Federal Security Bureau. 'What's the idea behind evacuating
children? Chechnya has been bled quite enough already without being

deprived of its children. How, what, on what basis?'

In the end I was forbidden to evacuate any children at all: 'Hands off our children!' In a word, everything the bureaucrats could do to foul the whole thing up with their press conferences, they did. With a great deal of difficulty, after meetings with Makhashev and Movsaev, I did get permission to evacuate at least the Russian children to safety. They said, 'On Tuesday at 14:00 hours a three-day supply of hot food, bed linen and clothing will be waiting for you in Sernovodsk at the Spas of the Caucasus sanatorium.' I had been to Sernovodsk during the war, and there hadn't been a brick left standing. I rushed to my Chechen friends. 'For pity's sake, give me a lift to Sernovodsk.' They said, 'Galina, you're crazy! We'd have to go through Samashki!' It was impossible for a Russian to pass through Samashki now. 'Well, perhaps we can get you through somehow.' I couldn't just take the children there without checking first. We got there. There wasn't just no food, there weren't even any cellars left! The next question was, why had they suggested sending the children here? The sanatorium director told me: 'The migration service of the Russian Federation gave orders to bring the children here so they could use them to get funds to restore the sanatorium.' That was one of the few occasions in the war when I burst into tears.

I went back to Moscow. The only thing I got Shamil to agree to was that he would allow me to evacuate Russian children whose relatives I managed to find. I placed a centre spread of photographs in *Moscow News*. For God's sake, identify your children!

I was called in by Victor Ilyushin again. He rang Panov, who was then Minister of Social Security. Later the ministry set up a Commission for the Orphaned Children of Grozny, and Panov said to me one time, 'You've got the children and we've got the commission. Let's go halves'. To my great good fortune Panov said the same thing to Ilyushin: 'We'll need funding', and all that. Ilyushin went purple and roared down the phone that first we should worry about the children; after that we could worry about chairs. I remembered that phrase. Then he sat down and looked very depressed.

So there we were. Everybody was running around doing nothing, and I had children barefoot in Grozny and it was December. I broadcast on Radio Echo of Moscow, appealing for people to bring whatever they could. I took two KamAZ trucks down to Grozny with aid. While they were thinking what to do I was at least giving the children, 132 of them, stockings for their feet. I went back to Moscow with another article about the children. This time the title was 'Terror against aid'. Now we were being prevented from giving aid: the children had become a valuable commodity. At first it had been possible to get them out on the quiet, but now Shamil had decided it would be neat to have his own corps of child soldiers just like Aushev. Not to mention the fact that they had started taking children who had been in the fighting from around Mata and Vedeno to terrorist training camps.

So I gave the children the charity clothing to wear, returned to Moscow, and wrote my piece. Ilyushin called me in again. He said, 'Galina Nikolaevna, I have read your latest article.' He must be positively the best read deputy prime minister in the world. I told him, 'You know, I've given up on your bureaucrats. The children are not going to survive the winter.' I had just been to the funeral of two little boys I had been hoping to evacuate, Sasha and Tolya Babichev. 'I've already lost two of the boys.' To which he said, 'What? Surely not! You mean children are dying!' He sat down and looked very depressed.

'Do you know who can help you? Can you go to Grozny tomorrow?' 'Yes.' 'I'll put you on Boris Berezovsky's plane.'

Berezovsky understood the score straight away. He said, 'I need some straightforward arithmetic: how much money you want and what you really need – a hospital, a sanatorium?' Of course, I explained all the difficulties to him. While we had been slowly getting things organised the situation had deteriorated. The children had become valuable, they were being hunted, everything had become more difficult. He said, 'If you are prepared to take on the responsibility, I will put up the money'. By now there was no longer any question of negotiating. We simply started shepherding together the children who, for the six months since August 1996, we had been feeding and clothing in Grozny.

The first to leave were a group of 10 children, including my own (although I didn't know at that time that they were going to end up being mine), the Fomichevs and Oparins. How did we get them out? We took the children outside 10 minutes before take-off and called the crews from Independent Television and Russian Radio and Television: 'For God's sake, turn on the cameras for 10 minutes, or they won't let us leave Grozny'. Sure enough, when the Chechens started threatening us with their rifles, one of the lads called out, 'Camera running!' They didn't know what to do and lowered the guns. The elections were the next day, I was going full speed ahead, and they didn't want the whole world to see them brandishing their automatic weapons at some lady and a crowd of children.

We had acted without any basis in law, and we still don't have one. I started doing the rounds of all the ministries, trying to get them to help. The Ministry of Education said 'Not our problem. We don't deal with orphans. Try the Ministry of Social Security.' The Ministry of Social Security said, 'Not our problem. Orphans have been taken over by the Ministry of Health, but yours are different orphans, so the competent body will be the Federal Migration Service.' When I went to the Federal Migration Service they told me, 'No, not us. We deal with refugees and displaced persons over 18 years of age who have parents. Your situation is not covered by any law. Anyway, the Ministry of Education should be dealing with them.' 'But they need a law then. Here they are. They seem to have been left off the list of the human race.' 'Better try the Ministry of Justice.'

Thank God for the Russian-American College where they teach orphaned children who have guardians. Even before I had managed to get birth certificates for them, a friend introduced me to the director of this college. She got in touch with her Americans, and they took the boys I was looking after to study there out of the goodness of their hearts. When the Americans heard the word 'Chechnya' and saw the children, they said, 'Of course, no problem. Sort yourself out in your own good time.' That was the only place nobody asked me for forms and certificates.

In total I evacuated 18 children. Not many, but now it is impossible to do more. ❏

Galina Mashtakova wrote this article for the forthcoming issue of Dos'e na Tsenzuru. *She died in October 1998*
Translated and edited from Dos'e *by Arch Tait*

EDWARD LUCIE-SMITH

Graft and graffiti

Two visits to Belgrade in quick succession, in early September and late November, straddling the Kosovo crisis, do little to clarify what must now be the most confusing political and cultural situation in Europe

Belgrade is a lively city. In the old part of town, on a long strip of land between the river Sava and the river Danube, the streets are full of people – and of cars. A Friday on the eve of a public holiday produces a massive traffic jam: the city gridlocks in a way reminiscent of Caracas or Saõ Paulo. There is clearly no lack of petrol and, while there are many rattletrap Yugos there are also appreciable numbers of high-end Mercedes and BMWs. The shop windows are full of goods, and many fascias bear international brand names: Versace, Armani, Levi Jeans. Yet this is a place under economic siege, subject to an international trade embargo. It has been estimated that as much as 25 per cent of the adult population is engaged in smuggling or some activity close to it.

It is also a city under a form of dictatorship, with an immense police force in proportion to the number of inhabitants. As many as one in eight adult Belgraders are policemen. Yet this police presence is very little felt. In the main shopping area, pedestrianised in the early 1980s, people stroll, chat, take the air, fill the street-side and open air cafés, sipping Belgrade's excellent coffee. The few visible policemen stroll with them in pairs. No-one gives them a second glance, and their body language says they are not expecting any trouble. Belgrade, at any rate in September, seems both safe and relaxed. Street crime appears to be almost non-existent. There are a few beggars, but no immediately visible prostitutes. The men standing slightly furtively on street-corners and at the entrances to alleyways are not drug-dealers but illegal money changers, whom the authorities appear to tolerate. The preferred currency is not dollars but Deutschmarks, though of all nationalities the

Headline: 'These papers have been suppressed for telling the truth!' – Credit ELS

Germans are perhaps the most unpopular. Germany's support for Croatia is a continuing irritant, often referred to, even by people who are, on the whole, reluctant to discuss politics.

By late November, after the Holbrooke-Milosevic deal on Kosovo, the situation has subtly deteriorated. The weather is much worse – from being unseasonably warm it has passed to being unseasonably cold. Stencilled protest graffiti representing a clenched fist have begun to appear in the underpasses that lead from the pedestrianised to the non-pedestrianised area. I hear that a handful of students have been arrested for making them, then held for 10 days incommunicado. The clenched fist emblem can also be found on badges – but these one can buy quite openly in the street. There is a new press law and small fly-posters have also started to appear in the underpasses. The headline is 'These papers have been suppressed for telling the truth!'. They share wall space with more numerous posters of the same sort advertising rock bands, *tai-chi* schools and tattoo parlours – these latter are often partly in English. Some people openly anticipate a new wave of street protests, like those that gained world attention in 1996-97. Others think that the disillusionment is too great, since it is a general perception that most of the original protest leaders have now sold out. In this sense, the atmosphere is a little like that in Paris following the *événements* of 1968.

Most of all, the impression is one of a society in many respects so traumatised by the catastrophic events of the 1990s that it no longer knows what direction to take. The symbol of this is the national holiday celebrating the Federation of Yugoslav Republics that falls on 29 November. Officially this remains the country's 'national day'. Everyone knows that it relates to something that no longer exists; no-one has any idea what to replace it with. The bitter irony of the occasion is not lost on Belgrade's quite numerous intellectuals. The country they now belong to is a torso from which the limbs have fallen one by one. The last remaining member of the Yugoslav Federation, the tiny Republic of Montenegro, no longer recognises many of the laws made by the central parliament, and looks as if it is about to secede. Kosovo is increasingly a no-go area for Serbs. This has both long- and short-term implications. First, because Kosovo is almost universally perceived as the historical heartland of Serbia – even though a shift in populations has placed Serbs in a minority there. Few Serbs, even the most liberal, are willing to contemplate giving it up entirely. Second, Milosevic's own rise to power was intimately linked to the demands he made, in the late 1980s, before he assumed the presidency, that the federal government reassert full control over the then quasi-independent regions of Vojvodina to the north and Kosovo to the south.

If Montenegro and Kosovo go, Serbia will be completely landlocked. It has already lost most of the former Yugoslav coastline to Croatia, and now faces East, rather than chiefly West as it did in Tito's day. One middle-aged professor spoke to me about the holidays he and his family used to take on the coast. 'You could pop across to Italy for lunch if you felt like it,' he said. 'I don't speak good Italian, but I speak enough to get around.' Underlying this was nostalgia not merely for the freedoms of the past, but for what now seems to many the golden age of Tito's sunset years, when people like himself were largely free to do as they liked.

Though he was in fact born a Croat, Tito's is the shadow that looms quite largely over present-day Serbia. His statues may have disappeared, but his spirit continues to haunt the psyches even of those Serbs who are too young really to remember him. One of the more amusing symptoms of this was an exhibition organised by the Soros-funded Center for Contemporary Art, one of a network of such art centres throughout Eastern Europe, at the museum built to house the trophies brought back by Tito from his triumphant visits abroad as leader of the so-called Non-Aligned Nations. It also contains – or contained – various bizarre goodies presented to him by a 'grateful' Yugoslavia, among them the fancy relay batons used by runners from various parts of the country on his official birthday. Since Tito's death in 1980, the building has usually been closed, and the more desirable items it contained are said to have been plundered by the present-day political elite for their own use. Now four young curators chosen by the Center for Contemporary Art have made an installation show featuring items from the collection, including rare examples of Socialist Realist art. The style was ephemeral in Yugoslavia, due to Tito's early break with Stalin, but one senses a kind of fascination with it among certain members of the current Serbian avant-garde. A similar fascination, more deeply rooted, is also manifesting itself among young avant-garde artists in Russia itself.

The Center forms part of an extremely lively intellectual scene in Belgrade. To intellectuals and artists, freedoms are allowed in non-political areas which in some respects exceed those available here in Britain. One such area is sexuality. Branislav Dimitrijevic, one of the programme coordinators at the Center, showed me a technically brilliant video made by a conceptual artist called Nesa Paripovic. It is an animation of Courbet's notorious painting *The Origin of the World,* which represents a woman's torso and sexual parts, seen in extreme close up. In the video the subject, following Maxime du Camp's excited contemporary description of the painting itself, is presented 'life-size, seen from the front, moved and convulsed, remarkably executed.' In Paripovic's version all the implications are spelt out: the torso slowly comes to life and the woman masturbates. I asked if there had been any trouble about showing this work. 'None here; there was a little when we showed it in Germany.'

But the Center is only one of a whole group of artistic institutions, often poorly funded but immensely active. My first visit to Belgrade was for a series of exhibitions of work by Radovan Kraguly, a Serbian-born artist with an international reputation who lives in Paris and in Wales. It occupied four different galleries in the centre of the city, two official, two unofficial. My second was to chair the jury for the Belgrade International Print Biennale, which was also surrounded by other satellite exhibitions, including one devoted to the Icelandic, but now international, Pop artist Erro and another to the Argentine Antoni Segui. City centre galleries always seem to be thronged.

This may sound as if the situation is more nearly normal artistically than in fact it is. Where the embargo seems to have had remarkably little effect from a practical point of view – though at a deeper level it distorts the Yugoslav economy at every point, encouraging a 'bandit' element which has increasing influence within the government itself – Serbian intellectuals clearly often feel they are stifling, deprived of the contacts that used to make Belgrade cosmopolitan. The current agitation as the government attempts to exert control over the universities was seen by a number (though certainly not by all) of the people I talked to as simply a battle between two political factions, neither of which deserved support. It conceals a much deeper dilemma, which is that of how to continue membership of a Europe-wide liberal consensus, in the face of the embargo and without ceasing to be Serbian. ❏

Edward Lucie-Smith is a UK-based writer and art critic. His latest books are Adam: the male nude *and* Zoo *(December 1998).* Women and Art: disputed territory, *written in collaboration with Judy Chicago (August 1999)*

ADAM MICHNIK

What sets Poles apart

Stefan Kisielewski (1911-1991) was a hugely successful journalist, essayist, politician, composer and novelist, and the literary *enfant terrible* of communist Poland. He wrote under a range of pseudonyms including Kisiel, Julia Holynska, Teodor Klon and Tomasz Stalinski; and though he was mostly in opposition to the Communist regime from the 1950s, the reasons weren't only political. Politics, morality, socialism and power were subjects of endless fascination. 'Poland has always had ideas too big for itself,' he once observed.

Despite limitations imposed by the censor, he managed to keep and publish a weekly diary with his personal observations of life under Stalinism which he dubbed 'the cult of the colossal'. During World War II he was publicly critical of the Polish tendency to idolise personal heroism and the military, and was accused of being a communist. Later, Marxists branded him a 'revolutionary' while Catholic colleagues referred to him as a 'capitalist' and, more accurately, a 'liberal'. He was a regular contributor to the widely read Catholic weekly *Tygodnik Powszechny*, published in Krakow.

His early novel *Sprzysiezenie* (Conspiracy, 1947) was well received by Marxist critics who, to Kisielewski's embarrassment, hailed him as an ally. Its hero, Zygmunt, founds a 'society for geniuses' along with two schoolfriends and swears with them to live by 'art, creativity and loyalty to nature' – all of which come down, in the end, to maintaining a celibate lifestyle. Of the three, one subsequently goes mad, another finds he is gay and Zygmunt becomes impotent, though he later recovers his manhood, fortuitously, amid the tribulations of war. The plot is complicated by another notional conspiracy to assassinate Hitler – though it's unclear if this is real or simply a figment of someone's imagination. The book's erotic content seemed bold for its times and it had a *succès de scandale*.

After the publication of further successful novels under the pseudonym Teodor Klon (including one which, like Venedikt Erofeev's *Moscow to Petushki*, reads like the autobiography of an alcoholic), Kisielewski muddied the waters further by publishing a novel in Paris under the pseudonym Tomasz Stalinski. *Widziane z góry* (Seen from the Top, 1963) detailed the personal and political peccadillos of a high-ranking politician in Poland and was a thinly disguised comment on the mechanisms of communist power, peopled with easily recognisable public figures. Immediately after its publication, there was much speculation on who the author might be; it was rumoured that Stanislaw Gomulka (then leader of the Polish Communist Party) had secret knowledge of his identity. The book was not published in Poland until 1989. Later novels by Stalinski published in the 1970s were less politically sensitive but continued to address topical issues such as the nationwide strikes in December 1970, and the mentality and ethics of the Polish intelligentsia.

Of the West, which he considered dull, Kisielewski remarked: 'They can say what they want, it's just that they've nothing to talk about.'

Czeslaw Milosz remarked that Stefan Kisielewski didn't understand the West. 'He had the mind of a "vieux Polonais", a patriot, a Sarmatian permanently foaming at the mouth. And you had to love him. You swallowed his prejudices whole.' Kisiel probably saw things differently. He was fascinated and infuriated by the West, because he saw it through the prism of Munich, Yalta, that strange 'Cold War' and even stranger 'Thaw'. He shaped himself against his times, he flew in the face of fashions, trends, salons or orthodoxy. He refused to conform; he was torn by anxiety and caught in the paradoxes of his own thinking, so opposed to the logic of his age. He belonged to the first generation of post-War Polish intellectuals, people like Milosz and Galczynski, Ksawery Pruszynski, Adolf Bochenski, Herling Grudzinski and Jerzy Turowicz.

People of that generation tried to overstep the debates they had inherited: all those rows between romantics and positivists, National Democrats and the supporters of Jozef Pilsudski. But they were the progeny of the very arguments they regarded as anachronistic. What was the significance, after all, of divisions between *sanacja* (the Pilsudski-ites) and national democrats, the right and the left, under the looming shadow of totalitarian dictatorship? Kisiel often demonstrated his dislike of stereotypical thinking – whether liberal left, National Democratic or conservative, concerning the planned economy, private ownership, social justice, US politics or, indeed, anti-semitism.

His sense of Polish identity ran deep. Perhaps because he understood its darker side. We often spoke of it. He disliked it when I poured scorn on Polish anti-semitism and – perhaps overzealously – pointed out the anti-semitic undertones in Party propaganda. 'Don't get involved,' he said, 'be careful!' He mentioned once that the Gestapo had entered his parents' house during the German Occupation. 'My father and I were afraid for my mother'. It was a throwaway line and I failed to understand. He looked at me suspiciously and muttered that his mother was Jewish.

Now I think that this is the key to understanding Kisiel. Stefan thought anti-semitism contemptible, but it was an issue he preferred to avoid. 'Don't get into this, it's not for you,' he'd say. On one occasion I got angry and retorted: 'Why me? Why won't you admit that it's not for either of us?'

He thought about it for a moment: 'Well, have it your way,' he conceded at last. 'I suppose it's not for either of us.' ...

The love he felt for Poland and the Poles was quite real, with no illusions. In his private diary he described the people of Warsaw's suburbs as 'ugly and graceless, neither peasants nor townspeople – thugs, if the truth be told.'

And here is an extract from his story 'Conspiracy', written under the German Occupation:

'People who genuinely interpret the history of the world as a demonic conspiracy by Jews who have control over the mechanisms of politics and economics, are like children whose over-active imagination looks for confirmation of fairytales in the world around them. A child is unaware that these fantasies will one day seem as colourless as they are cheap, and that only then will the full spectrum of life's mystery be revealed. Jews don't rule the world. Jews aren't guilty of everything, Jewish people aren't uniform or unanimously in agreement about things. Nor are they demonic, mysterious, exotic, strange and terrible. Jews are ordinary: the guilty and the innocent, the mad, the sane, the sly and the naïve. Only the crude sensuality and naïvety of public perception has made a myth of them.

'Zygmunt often thought about this strange, anti-semitic mysticism, whose fanatical adherents he met at university. They were frequently well educated, hard-working, self-denying, disinterested – men of ideas. Their mysticism undoubtedly had a magic and intensity which rehabilitated it up to a point, and made it measurable in terms of "spirituality", though it sprang from absurdity and incorporated an agenda full of brutality and cruelty. But what Zygmunt found completely vile, charmless and inexplicable was that passive, instinctive closet anti-semitism with no framework, seeking no intellectual or spiritual vindication, which arbitrarily released a brutal loathing for something alien or different, that passionate hatred and subconscious envy of a foreign life, a foreign vitality, a foreign mobility. This was deep-rooted in Poland. Zygmunt concluded that a brutality and ruthlessness towards Jews was something potentially concealed in almost every ordinary Pole.

'He understood this following an incident he witnessed while going on holiday from the cadet school (*podchorazowka*) with a group of friends. They were all the sons of well-to-do people, cultured, reasonably well-read, with perfect social skills. At one of the stations, the door of the compartment opened and a lovely dark-eyed girl appeared asking if a place was free. Zygmunt's friends greeted her enthusiastically, a space was vacated, one of them even helped her up the steps of the railway carriage. But then someone noticed that she was Jewish. Without more ado, her suitcase was despatched through the window and she was pushed off the train which was already picking up speed. Zygmunt was shaken. It was an event which opened his eyes to astonishing and unfamiliar recesses in the psychology of his contemporaries. But he kept silent and showed nothing, though later he blamed himself for cowardice or opportunism coming from a fear of alienating his friends. After that, he always demonstrated his sympathy for the Jews, which frequently brought him unpleasantness and pain.'

It would be hard to give a clearer diagnosis of the chronic anti-semitism which poisons the Polish mind. Yet after the war, Kisiel was circumspect about the subject and touched it seldom. Why?

He told me once that in the 1950s, after a *feuilleton* published in *Tygodnik Powszechny*, he received several anonymous letters reminding him of his mother's Jewish origins. And that was when I understood that this spectacularly brave man was afraid of just one thing: that he'd be attacked as a Jew. Stefan was prepared to answer for anything he said, wrote or did. But he didn't want to be branded for having a mother of the wrong origin. He sensed a trap. He refused to accept that a grain of anti-semitism is the hallmark of 'being Polish'. But nor did he want to be categorised in racist terms.

Kisiel played with 'being Polish', and he did so with genius. But he knew these were dangerous games. ...

He resolved his personal conundrum – that of being a man who constantly contested everything and everyone – by making a case for tolerance. 'An indulgent human being can still regard many views as mistaken and many actions as nefarious, and has a duty to fight them, because to be tolerant is not to be a sceptic without views. A tolerant human being shouldn't fantasise about things that are evil or wrong vanishing overnight or never existing at all. Tolerance acknowledges that every mistaken view or evil deed, which is a travesty or contradiction of truth, is nevertheless dependent on truth, because negation is a form of dependence and confirms the existence of the true. Without truth there would be no falsehood. As long as human beings exist they will continue to give this inverted witness to truth, affirming it through denial, because you can only deny what exists. A tolerant person knows that to be uncompromising in the fight for truth is still to retain an indulgence of the heart towards human falsehood. A human being can legitimately conquer and tame but never, legitimately, judge.'

Stefan Kisielewski didn't judge. Only today, reading those old *feuilletons,* do we call on his wisdom to do so. We perceive and recognise our own wretchedness and frailty through the reflected splendour of his spirit. ❏

Adam Michnik is the editor-in-chief of the Polish daily Gazeta Wyborcza
Translated by Irena Maryniak

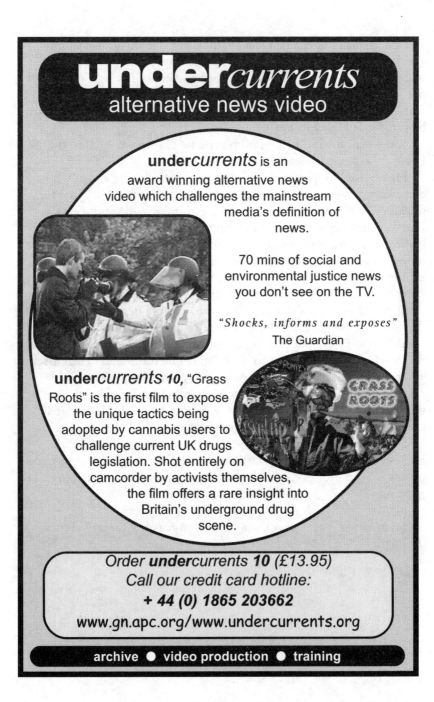

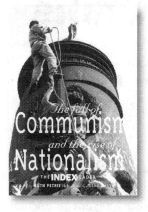

JULIAN PETLEY

SLAPPS and Chills

This year's round-up of television troubles concentrates specifically on the bullying of broadcasters and asks: are they being SLAPPed around?

SLAPPS stands for Strategic Lawsuits against Public Participation. The term was first coined by two US academics who noticed that powerful corporate interests were increasingly threatening environmental campaigners with lawsuits for defamation, conspiracy, invasion of privacy, interference with business and so on. These cases rarely came to court, but nor were they intended to; rather, SLAPPS are a form of strategic legal intimidation or gamesmanship, designed to frighten, harass and distract actual critics, and to discourage potential ones from even voicing their views in the first place. Is this tactic now spreading from the USA and beyond the environmental arena? Let's have a look at the broadcasting year in this particular light.

Certainly, those covering environmental protests are increasingly feeling the heavy hand of the law. Indeed so serious is the situation that Patricia McKenna, a UK Member of the European Parliament, has tabled a question at the European Parliament accusing the police of mistreating members of the National Union of Journalists 'by not recognising their Press Cards, arresting them for trespass or obstruction or even, under the Harassment Act (intended to prevent stalking), assaulting them, holding them until deadlines are passed, preventing them from taking pictures, confiscating their photographs with court orders, and erasing their video material, as well as restricting their public access during protests' (*Index* 5/98, see also Undercurrents 9 'Breaking News').

This year a charge of obstruction against a student cameraman covering the 1997 Manchester Airport protest for Channel 5's *What's the*

Story? came to light in January when it was dropped after the Crown Prosecution Service offered no evidence, but in August Ben Edwards of Eye Contact, a Bristol video news agency, was arrested while filming a demonstration at a genetically modified maize site in south Devon. While he was under arrest, his house was searched by Bristol police who removed computer disks, documents and tapes. He was released on bail without charge, but his equipment remained confiscated in what can only be construed as a crude attempt to put him out of business.

Meanwhile, Roddy Mansfield, a video journalist with the Oxford-based Undercurrents group, has been arrested no fewer than six times and, with the aid of the NUJ, is now suing the Metropolitan Police. No wonder we see so little coverage of environmental protests on television.

A classic SLAPPS story emerged in June 1997, when Franny Armstrong revealed that both Channel 4 and the BBC were unwilling to show her remarkable film *McLibel: Two Worlds Collide* for fear of – yes, you guessed – libel. (*Index* 5/98). And this in spite of the fact that the once notoriously litigious McDonalds appears to have been somewhat chastened by their lengthy and bruising court encounter with Helen Steel and Dave Morris. Still, as long as broadcasters tremble at the burger giant's erstwhile fearsome reputation, the SLAPP syndrome is still doing its dirty work.

Photographer Nick Cobbing, arrested covering Oxford animal rights demo, December 1998 – Credit: Andrew Testa

In March, a real live libel case came, albeit very briefly, to court, with Marks and Spencer versus Granada over the 1996 *World in Action* programme 'St Michael: Has the Halo Slipped?' which revealed that one of their Moroccan suppliers exploited child labour and labelled garments 'Made in England'. M&S insisted that the programme implied that it knew of these abuses; Granada denied this and argued that the programme demonstrated merely that the company had failed to monitor its suppliers properly. On the first day of what was expected to be a long and complex trial, Mr Justice Popplewell simply asked the jury whether they thought 'Mr Average Viewer' would have taken the programme to mean what M&S claimed it meant. After a short deliberation the jury supported the M&S interpretation, and Granada, not permitted to present any evidence in its defence, was forced to concede and to pay £700,000 (cUS$1.2 m) in costs and damages.

This 'sudden death' procedure may cut legal costs by avoiding lengthy libel trials, but such a crudely 'common-sensical' approach is hardly best suited to settling highly complex matters of fact and interpretation. Britain's libel laws which, unlike those of many other countries, place the onus on the defendant to prove truth or show fair comment, not only put the defendant at a considerable disadvantage vis-à-vis the plaintiff, they already exert what has been called a considerable 'chilling effect' on investigative journalism. This latest judgement threatens to lower the temperature to freezing point. As Ian McBride, Granada's managing editor of factual programmes put it: 'To have to ponder and second guess our fate in a short-cut route through the libel roulette puts another burden and potential hazard in the way of inquiring, challenging journalism and the communication of important, if uncomfortable, truths to the public'.

Corporate players in this game have also been busily exploiting the various broadcasting complaints systems. In February, the BBC *Programme Complaints Bulletin* revealed that a number of complaints from Sir Richard Evans, chief executive of British Aerospace, about a June 1997 *Newsnight* report on the Eurofighter, had been upheld. In this context it's also worth noting that in December 1997, British Aerospace had refused to co-operate with, and then threatened to sue, a *Panorama* programme on the same subject.

Just how sensitive big business has become to journalistic scrutiny was revealed in August when the chairmen of ten of the country's biggest companies, including, apparently – 'apparently' since the 'Watchdog Ten' are peculiarly coy about their composition and activities – Ford, the AA, Airtours, BT, DSG Retail (owners of the retail chains Dixons and PC World), Hotpoint and Procter and Gamble, met to discuss a plan of campaign against the BBC's Watchdog.

Since developing its journalistic teeth, the programme has not shirked taking on the big High Street names, including the above, and the response has been a barrage of complaints, 12 of which have been upheld by the Programme Complaints Unit over the past four years. It's also worth noting that this year the Broadcasting Standards Commission has entertained (and upheld or partly upheld) complaints about Watchdog from Ford, Dixons and Airtours. Another busy corporate complainant to both the BSC and the Independent Television Commission has been Barratt Developments, a construction company that seems to be particularly sensitive to programmes about houses it has built on brown field [formerly industrial or derelict land] sites.

Nobody, of course, can or should defend stories that don't stand up. However, whether the above examples constitute proper use of the complaints systems – especially if complaints are accompanied by threats of legal action – is certainly open to question. Furthermore, ever since the crucial 1993 action between Derbyshire County Council and Times Newspapers, a public authority in Britain cannot bring a libel action because this would inhibit freedom of political speech. Yet, as the powers of public authorities, including governments, daily drain away, and those of big business increase in direct proportion, there is certainly an argument that the definition of what actually constitutes 'political speech' needs to be widened.

It could convincingly be argued that the major political forces in the world today are no longer national governments but transnational corporations. In such a situation, and especially given large companies' increasing willingness to resort to SLAPPs and other 'chilling' tactics, is it not time that their legal arsenal was depleted? Would not taking away their much-abused ability to exploit our oppressive and archaic libel laws be an excellent place to start? They do, after all, have other means with which to defend themselves. ❏

Julian Petley writes regularly for Index *on film and video. He is a lecturer in Media and Communication Studies at Brunel University*

SUPPORT FOR
INDEX

Credit: Sisi Burn

Index on Censorship would like to thank the following for their generous contributions to the *evening of banned music* and *Smashed Hits:*

Stephen Spender Memorial Fund
The Golsoncot Foundation
John McFadden
Carlton Television

The concert committee
The John S Cohen Foundation
The *Express* Group Newspapers

The Trustees and Directors would like to thank the many individuals and organisations who support *Index on Censorship* and the *Writers and Scholars Educational Trust (WSET)*, including :

Anonymous
The Ajahma Charitable Trust
The Arts Council of England
The Bromley Trust
Danish International Development Agency
(DANIDA)
Demokratifonden
The European Commission
The Ford Foundation
Fritt Ord Foundation
The JM Kaplan Fund
The Goldberg Family Trust
The Lyndhurst Settlement
Neda
The Onaway Trust
The Open Society Institute

Pearson plc Charitable Trust
The Prins Claus Fund
The Ruben and Elisabeth Rausing Trust
CA Rodewald Charitable Settlement
EJB Rose Charitable Trust
The Royal Literary Fund
The Royal Ministry of Foreign Affairs, Norway
The Alan and Babette Sainsbury Charitable
Fund
Scottish Media Group plc
Tom Stoppard
Swedish International Development
Cooperation Agency (Sida)
UNESCO
United News and Media plc

If you would like more information about *Index on Censorship* or would like to support our work, please contact *Index* on
(44) 171 278 2313 or e-mail contact@indexoncensorship.org